1, November, 1991

Sharon,
   How lovely having a
"Baroness" as a friend. We
wish you great success!
      Love,
      Lyn & Russ

AN ENGLISH COUNTRY LADY'S

BOOK OF

DRIED FLOWERS

AN ENGLISH COUNTRY LADY'S

BOOK OF

DRIED FLOWERS

AMANDA DOCKER

Flowers with Simon Lycett

DOUBLEDAY

NEW YORK · LONDON · TORONTO · SYDNEY · AUCKLAND

Design by Polly Dawes
Photographs by Julie Fisher
Styling by Jacky Boase

PUBLISHED BY DOUBLEDAY
a division of Bantam Doubleday Dell Publishing Group Inc.,
666 Fifth Avenue, New York, New York 10103

DOUBLEDAY and the portrayal of an anchor
with a dolphin are trademarks of Doubleday,
a division of Bantam Doubleday Dell Publishing Group, Inc.

Originally published in Great Britain as *Armscote Manor
Book of Dried Flowers* by Century Editions, an imprint
of The Random Century Group Ltd, in 1990

Library of Congress Cataloging-in-Publication Data

Docker, Amanda.
An English country lady's book of dried flowers/
Amanda Docker – 1st ed. in the U.S.A.
p.   cm.
1. Dried flower arrangement. 2. Flowers – Drying. I. Title.
SB449.3.D7D63 1990
745.92 – dc20   89-49469
CIP

ISBN 0-385-41359-9

Typeset in Great Britain by SX Composing Ltd, Rayleigh, Essex
Colour separation by Colorlito, Milan
Printed and bound in Spain by Printer Industria Gráfica, Barcelona

PROP ACKNOWLEDGEMENTS

The author and publishers are grateful to the following companies for
the loan of items used in the photographs for this book.

James Davis
Pine and Country Antiques
28 Church Street
Shipton-on-Stour

Gallery of Antique Costume and Textiles
2 Church Street
Marylebone
London NW8

For Fred, who is such a great business mentor, guide and
motivator, and my patient and understanding family –
especially my mother, whose garden I've robbed of
flowers on many occasions.

ACKNOWLEDGEMENTS

Grateful thanks are due to the many people who have made vital contributions to this book, but especially to:

All my wonderful friends who so kindly allowed us into their homes – Jane Brabyn, Dominic and Sally Cadbury, George and Caroline Docker, Robert and Fiona Grant, the Sandiford family, Michael and Louise Wigley, the Reverend Roger Williams, rector of St James the Great, Idlicote and last (but not least!) Charlie and Julie. Thanks, too, to Karen Abel-Smith for help in finding locations.

The Armscote Manor Dried Flowers workforce, who took all requests in their stride. Special thanks to the invaluable Mary Davis, who always keeps everything running smoothly, to Mick for solving so many practical problems and to Liz in the office.

The floristry team who helped with and inspired so many of the arrangements – the brilliant Simon Lycett, Antony Mifsud who created the arrangements on pages 37, 61, 62 and the central arrangement on pages 20-21, and David Greenwood and Annie Daniels.

Everyone who supplied materials for the arrangements, including Lady Beecham for the wonderful artichokes, Kari Dill for leek heads, Hamish Greycheap for the splendid Christmas tree, Jenny Henstock and Anne Davenport for their lovely stone and terracotta pots and Miss Williams for the honesty.

James Davis of Pine and Country Antiques for lending us so many antiques.

Gyles and Michele Brandreth for getting the whole project off the ground.

Julie Fisher and her assistants for the lovely pictures, Jacky Boase for styling them and Mary Douglas for help with writing and transport.

June for all the lunches and bed changing!

And, finally, to my family for putting up with all the disruption during the making of this book.

CONTENTS

CHAPTER ONE

A WALK AROUND ARMSCOTE MANOR

Armscote Manor is set in the gently rolling countryside of the northern Cotswolds, surrounded by gardens that have scarcely changed since the house was built at the end of the sixteenth century. Today, as well as being our family home, it's the centre of one of the largest dried-flower businesses in Britain. In the barns and outhouses around the stableyard are workrooms where flowers are transformed into arrangements and sold the world over. Let me introduce you to the place and its history, and to some of the people who live and work there . . .

Armscote Manor, our home and the inspiration for our dried-flower business. In the foreground is a selection of the arrangements we make there.

THE FLOWERS OF THE FIELD

The little history we know of Armscote Manor begins in 1587, when John Halford inherited the original house and its lands from his father. Armscote must have taken the latter part of its name from the sheep-cotes that dotted the fields all over the area that, because of them, became known as the Cotswolds. In the sixteenth century Cotswold wool was considered the finest in Europe and it was probably on wool that the Halfords' fortunes were founded.

During the 13 years between inheriting the manor and the end of the century, John Halford built the house that my husband Fred, my children Sophie and William, and I live in today. When he carved his initials into the oak front door the wood must have been new and still soft enough to be worked. Nearly 400 years later it is black and hardened with age, but his initials are still there.

There are other strands from the past that reach out to us across the centuries. While John Halford was building his new house at Armscote, a local man, William Shakespeare from Stratford-upon-Avon, just ten miles up the road, was making his name in London. Today, I need hardly point out, Shakespeare is still Stratford's biggest claim to fame.

Another link that I like to imagine ties the house as it is now to the house as it was then, concerns Halford's wife. When the Halfords moved into their home they would very probably have used dried and preserved flowers to scent the rooms. Perhaps Mrs Halford and her servants spent their summers drying herbs and lavender, which would have been burnt to perfume the house when dampness made it musty – the word 'perfume', incidentally, coming from the Latin meaning 'through smoke'. Perhaps she collected petals from the rose garden at the back of the house and used them to make the delicious moist potpourri, at that time literally a 'putrid pot', that was the precursor of today's dry potpourri. Maybe she dried sprigs of tansy, wormwood, rosemary and lavender and hung them in bunches in cupboards to deter moths from the Cotswold woollens. Indeed she may have dried other garden flowers so that they could be used to brighten the house during the long, dark days of winter.

I hope she did, because it pleases me to think that after four centuries dried flowers still play a significant part in the life of Armscote Manor. True, our closets don't contain bunches of wormwood and rosemary to keep away the moths, but our rooms are perfumed with potpourri and we still, each year, dry roses, lavender, herbs and many other flowers picked from the gardens the Halfords knew. Whether this traditional use of flowers was observed throughout the intervening years, we'll unfortunately never know. The Halfords lived quiet lives and quiet lives tend to be overlooked by history.

Armscote is said to have provided a hiding-place for Guy Fawkes, who attempted to blow up the Houses of Parliament in 1605. Unfortunately he is said to have stayed in so many other houses in the area that it's something of a local joke.

History does, however, record one incident that occurred at the manor on 17 December 1673. The generation of Halfords then living at Armscote were religious non-conformists and when George Fox, founder and

Hollyhocks outside the front door where John Halford, the man who built Armscote Manor, carved his initials. My companion is Teal, our golden retriever.

leader of the Quakers, was travelling from London to his home in the North of England they offered him accommodation at the manor. That evening a meeting was arranged and so many local people flocked to attend that it had to be held in the barn. Fox tells the story in his journal:

We . . . went to John Halford's, at Armscot in Tredington parish, where we had a very large and precious meeting in his barn, the Lord's powerful presence being amongst us.

After the meeting, Friends being most of them gone, as I was sitting in the parlour, discoursing with some Friends that staid, one Henry Parker, called a justice, came to the house, and with him one Rowland Hains, a priest of Honington, in Warwickshire.

Parker and Hains arrested Fox and took him to Worcester Jail, from where he was later released to continue his work. The incident was never forgotten, however, and to this day local Quakers commemorate the event by coming to lunch at Armscote on the first day of August each year and walking in the gardens where Fox once walked. The Halfords' faith may well explain why we know so little about them. As Quakers they would have pursued neither fame nor fortune – and it is perhaps as a consequence of the latter that the manor eventually passed out of their hands.

It came into ours in 1977, in need of restoration after an unsympathetic Victorian treatment that had tried to conceal the real character of the place. Fred and I lived in a cottage nearby for a year while the architects and builders did their best to uncover what original features remained. The fireplaces were still there, and some of the flagstones, but we never quite managed to work out which area would have been the high-ceilinged Elizabethan hall that is so characteristic of houses from this period. We moved in just before our son, William, was born.

Having found ourselves a beautiful home, Fred and I now had to work out a way of keeping it. With the house

had come 16 acres of land and a full-time gardener, both of which needed to be put to good use. Fred is the business brains of the family, and his entrepreneurial instincts guided us in the direction of dried flowers. We decided to grow and dry our own and make them into arrangements which we would then sell by mail order. And I would be in charge of the day-to-day business.

Becoming a businesswoman was the last thing I had anticipated and not a prospect I welcomed with much warmth. Before our marriage I'd worked with horses and they were my only real interest outside the family. My idea of a good time was (and still is) to go riding or salmon fishing in Scotland. Business meetings, spread sheets and cash-flow projections were not something I felt terribly confident about, but with Fred's constant guidance and assistance, Armscote Manor Dried Flowers was established in 1979.

Not the least of my concerns was the fact that I had no training in floristry. Many people assume that I'm a professional or that at the very least I'd gone to the kind of school where flower arranging was taught. I didn't, and qualifications in Maths, Zoology and Geography were not much use when it came to designing our first products. Fortunately we were lucky to find a very skilled and imaginative florist living in the next village and she helped us tremendously. It was from her that I learned all my basic skills. I'm sure now that it was an advantage not to have been formally trained. If you don't know the 'rules' of

Off to another Pony Club gymkhana. My children have inherited my love of horses and we often spend our weekends riding. Here's Sophie with her pony Bruni and William with Minnie. Unfortunately Fred was too busy mucking out the horse box to be in the picture.

*Fiona, one of our wonderful team
of arrangers, making a special
commission in the workroom*

dried flower arranging, then you have no inhibitions about breaking them!

The early years of the company were exciting and, sometimes, disastrous. Our gardener certainly knew how to grow the flowers we needed, but we had frequent problems with fields of flowers destroyed by rain or mildew. On one memorable occasion a whole crop of helichrysums was wiped out by leatherjackets. Setbacks aside, the fields full of flowers were a glorious sight and it was wonderful to be out on summer mornings picking them – even if our gardener's idea of a practical joke was to fasten my brimming basket to the ground with a length of wire so that when I tried to pick it up everything fell out!

The barn that we converted to a drying shed was a magnificent sight, with racks of flowers strung up to the ceiling and everywhere great masses of colour and foliage. Helping to run all this and turn the dried flowers into finished arrangements was a team of workers recruited from the local area.

From these small and perhaps unlikely beginnings, the business grew. We reduced the amount of trade done through mail order because of problems with packing and transporting the individual arrangements and instead began selling in bulk to retailers. As the number of orders grew, so did the problem of producing enough flowers for them. An ever-increasing amount of material had to be brought in from outside and we needed extra space to store it. As word of us spread, local arrangers and shops began asking if we could supply them with flowers. People began to call at the manor to buy arrangements or to ask us to make special commissions for them. If our business was to expand, we would have to make some changes.

Reluctantly we decided that it simply wasn't practical to go on growing and drying our own materials. We needed the barn for more work-rooms, and to create a

A small sample of the flowers and materials on sale at the Armscote Manor shop. We stock flowers to suit all tastes, including exotic proteas and banksias, but our best-sellers are traditional pink roses. When we started the business in 1979 there was a relatively limited range of flowers available. Today exotic material comes to us from all over the world. We in turn export our arrangements throughout Europe and to places as far afield as Barbados, Bermuda, the United States, Japan and even the Falkland Islands.

showroom and shop where our flowers could be displayed. It's rather sad that today's arrangements aren't made from flowers grown at Armscote, but we still have local people who supply us. Ewan Evans is the most remarkable of our suppliers. He grows and individually wires up all the helichrysums we use – and we use lots. He also cooks a brilliant breakfast when he comes with us to trade fairs! Other friends kindly grow or collect other sorts of material, including such things as artichokes and onion heads. One of my mother's friends collects fir cones and larch twigs for us, invaluable for our Christmas arrangements.

The fields around the manor may no longer be full of flowers, but the garden certainly is, and most of them can be dried. Every year I cut armfuls of each variety and hang them in the kitchen or, when there are too many to cope with there, in the loft above the work-rooms. When they are dry I use them for my own arrangements.

We regularly arrange evening visits to Armscote for groups who are interested in dried flowers and when the weather is good enough I begin by inviting them to walk around the gardens with me. As we go I point out all the materials that can be dried. Later we return to the work-room for a demonstration and there I sometimes make an arrangement incorporating dried flowers from one of the flowerbeds we have just seen. Our visitors often go away full of new ideas and plans for their own gardens. If you are interested in growing flowers to dry, I've drawn up a list of the most common and suitable garden flowers on page 140. And on page 130 you will find details of the various methods that can be used to dry them. It's worth doing, even though it's so easy to buy commercially-grown dried flowers. There's something very satisfying about making arrangements from materials you have cultivated and preserved yourself.

We are planning some changes in the garden. To one side of the house is the old, walled, kitchen garden. We call it the moon garden because one way of entering it is via a circular archway, like a moon. Here we used to grow flowers for havesting, but for the last year or two it has been allowed a rest from intensive cultivation. It's here that we are planning a show garden of annuals, perennials and everything that can be grown for drying. The traditional English garden flowers – peonies, delphiniums, the different varieties of roses, poppies, achilleas, alchemilla, hydrangeas, sedum, anaphalis and on down an almost endless list – will be cultivated and we may also attempt to grow some of the more exotic and unusual plants that can be dried. We hope that this will provide our visitors with some extra inspiration.

I'm sometimes asked about my personal preferences when it comes to flowers. Personally I love informality; wild flowers, herbs and old-fashioned garden flowers, fresh or dried, are my favourites. I like natural, loose-looking bunches and arrangements with lots of seed heads and contrasts. Often the simplest arrangement, perhaps a container filled with just one variety of flower, can look spectacular. I admire the flair of European arrangers, who are more bold and daring than the traditional English school of floristry, which tends to stiffness and pointed triangular shapes. That said, I'm not a great fan of the wildly modern, brightly-coloured arrangements one sees in Europe, full of dyed flowers and odd accessories. Like so many other English people I love a natural, informal style of gardening, full of soft, rich colours and shapes, and I prefer my flower arrangements to echo that style.

It delights me that after so many years of decline, the art of producing and arranging dried flowers has made its comeback. For centuries people preserved and dried flowers to create a reminder of summer through the long winter, but in this century the practice seemed in danger of dying out. One of the most encouraging developments since Armscote Manor Dried Flowers began trading has been the huge increase in the varieties of flowers available on the market, with new additions every year.

Of course, no dried material can rival the delicacy of fresh flowers. A solitary dried rose will never arouse quite the same feelings as a perfect fresh one. But there's tremendous satisfaction to be derived from preserving the beauty of flowers by drying them and then making them into a wonderful arrangement, a permanent reminder of their impermanent beauty.

Whilst a bunch of beautiful fresh flowers needs very little effort to make it look good, dried flowers require more time and, most of all, inspiration. All too often, even today when there are so many excellent dried-flower suppliers around, people's idea of an arrangement is a few hydrangeas grouped with some statice or honesty in a vase. No one could begin to pretend that this kind of treatment does anything to enhance the look of the flowers, the vase or the setting. For dried flowers to look their best they need to be selected and arranged with a theme or an idea in mind that has been inspired by the setting in which they will be seen. In this way the flowers, setting and container will complement each other and the arrangement becomes not just a decoration, but an important and beautiful feature of the room.

To demonstrate how this works in practice, I'd like to take you on a tour of the lovely Cotswold homes of my friends and family and show you some of the magical qualities of dried flowers and the tremendous variety of materials available for use. If you're new to flowers and flower arranging don't be put off by the terrifying Latin names accorded to some of the plants. Wherever possible I've used their more familiar titles, but certain species are only known in their Latin form, so in these instances, I've had to give the Latin. On the journey I'll explain the sources of our inspiration and the thinking behind the arrangements. I'll outline the basic skills involved and pass on the tips I've learned over my years at Armscote Manor. I hope what you see and read will inspire you to make new and imaginative arrangements of your own. Forget the rules, the traditional colour combinations and the established ways of doing things. Just follow your creative instincts and enjoy the results.

CHAPTER TWO
AROUND THE HOME

Dried flowers are often viewed in a purely practical light, as nothing more than a convenient way of decorating a stark corner or a bare piece of furniture. But used with imagination they can become a beautiful and integral feature in the design of any room, and give enduring pleasure throughout the year. Come with me to visit the homes of some of my friends and let me show you how dried flowers make them such beautiful places to live . . .

Dried flowers are the perfect complement to the mature colours and textures of old terracotta tiles and mellow wooden furniture

KITCHENS AND CORNERS

According to some authorities dried flowers aren't a practical proposition in kitchens, utility rooms and other places around the house where water, steam, intense heat and bustling activity create exactly the kind of conditions guaranteed to ruin them. And certainly, if your kitchen steams up each time you boil the kettle, or is so small there's nowhere but the draining board on which to put an arrangement then you're unlikely to find that dried flowers last long or look good.

But as I know from my own experience, some kitchens can be ideal locations for dried flowers. At Armscote we're fortunate enough to have an Aga, an absolute godsend for anyone who likes to dry their own flowers. There's usually a whole rack of flowers freshly cut above mine, and when they're dry – often just a matter of a few days – I hang them in bunches from the beams across the ceiling until they're used. In summer we breakfast under roses, peonies, alchemilla and artichokes, to name just a few of the things I pick from the garden. At other times of the year visitors find herbs and greenery gently drying over their heads.

Many kitchens in older country houses, my own included, face north and can be rather gloomy. But what's bad news for the cook is good news for dried flowers, for they keep their colour best when they're out of direct sunlight. Nothing could suit them better than a shady kitchen with plenty of dry heat, and they'll do wonders for the look of the room, particularly if it's decorated and furnished in a country style.

There can be few more delightful kitchens than the one shown on the previous page. The owners of the house are great Francophiles who love the warmth and simplicity of Provençal style and have recreated it in their Oxfordshire home. This is the kind of kitchen in which dried flowers are indispensable, and we created three highly individual arrangements to complement its character.

On the left of the picture is a tall basket, loosely filled with dried herbs including rosemary, bay, lavender, marjoram, tansy, curry plant, feverfew, borage, catmint, sage and chive flowers. They were all freshly dried, having been picked only a week or so earlier, and were pungent enough to scent the entire room and give it an earthy, appetizing aroma. We picked the herbs at a growers' not far from Armscote and discovered that the flowers are usually cut and thrown away because they cannot be processed. If you'd like a similar arrangement of your own but don't have a herb garden, you might try approaching your local herb nursery and asking if you may pick a few armfuls of flowers. You may find that you're doing them a favour.

Heads of garlic and *bouquets garnis* were wired over the rim and down the sides of the basket, adding to the aromatic dimension of the arrangement. The technique for attaching the garlic or, indeed, any other type of fruit or vegetable, is quite simple. Run a heavy-gauge florists' wire (see page 134) through either end of the bulb, twist the wire firmly round the base of the garlic to hold it in place, and then thread the ends into position through the basket and secure. For an almost instant transformation of a plain basket, ready-made plaits of garlic can be wired around the edges, as demonstrated in the picture. Garlic will look good for many months until it dries out and discolours, at which point it can easily be replaced with new bulbs. With the *bouquets garnis* it's an important addition to this design not just because of its aroma but because it helps break up the line between the basket and the flowers

Few arrangements could be more appropriate in the kitchen than dried herbs, which fill the room with a pungent and pleasing fragrance. Grow your own herbs for drying or ask a herb grower if you can cut flowers in the summer.

to create an attractive and fully integrated arrangement.

On the low painted chest, beneath the flying angel, is an intriguing arrangement made of twigs and knobbly-textured banana sticks, with a green background of cartha-mus. It's like a fantasy tree, with walnuts, pecan nuts and tiny terracotta flowerpots, only an inch or two in diameter, clustered among the branches, while larch cones, tama-rind husks and the muted pink *Protea sulphurea* add colour and texture at the base. This is a fun arrangement, eccentric and eclectic, full of new discoveries each time one looks at it. Gnarled old apple twigs would make an equally interesting framework for the arrangement, and one could fill the small pots with dried-flower heads for a softer and more colourful approach. Dried acorns and prickly chestnuts would also look good.

Seeking inspiration for the third arrangement, we asked ourselves what kind of images were conjured up by thoughts of a warm country kitchen. Freshly baked bread came immediately to mind – and there it was, our theme. I find this kind of brainstorming technique immensely useful when I'm searching for new ideas. Even if the first idea that comes to you doesn't appear to have anything to do with dried flowers, it's worth trying to incorporate it into an arrangement. You may be pleasantly surprised at the results.

We filled an old terracotta breadcrock (borrowed from my mother and still, I confess, to be returned) with upright wheat stalks. Then a moss garland was attached around the rim of the crock using strong florists' tape (see page 134), which is invaluable for fixing materials to solid containers that you don't want to damage. If you're attaching a garland permanently and aren't concerned about damaging the container then use glue – if possible hot glue, applied with a glue gun, which gives the best adhesion. Into the garland were wired a number of bread rolls

Imagination and wit – two of the key words when it comes to creating truly original designs. Here, bread rolls and kitchen implements transform a very simple arrangement into something that's different, fun, and perfect for its setting.

of different shapes and sizes. Bread will last almost indefinitely in an arrangement as long as it is kept in dry conditions, otherwise it will go mouldy. If you want to preserve it allow it to dry in the air for a few days and then spray it with clear varnish. Then we added an assortment of small and interesting kitchen implements. Our housekeeper, June, arrived for work the next day to discover that most of her wooden spoons had mysteriously disappeared. A sugar shaker, pastry cutters, cornet tins, little madeleine moulds and butter pats were all included. To finish the garland off, small bunches of wheat were interspersed among the utensils, hiding any wires and providing a visual link with the sheaf above.

I should, perhaps, sound a light-hearted note of caution about arrangements incorporating edible materials such as the loaves used here. Be careful if you have hungry dogs (or even, for that matter, hungry children) about. We left this arrangement, complete with bread, on the kitchen floor overnight. Teal, our golden retriever, was unable to resist the temptation, and when we came down in the morning all the rolls had gone.

Kitchens aren't the only functional rooms in the house that can be dressed-up with a dried arrangement. This hall-turned-boot-room, for example, made an excellent setting for one of the standard arrangements we produce at Armscote. I call it the Becher's Brook because the twig-covered basket and shape remind me of the formidable steeplechase fence of the same name in the Grand National. It is one of our best-selling styles and popular, I suspect, not only because it looks good but because it is narrow and flat-backed, which makes it useful for placing against walls. This is a particular bonus in narrow halls and landings, where there's less likelihood of it being knocked over by someone accidentally brushing past.

There's not much danger of that happening here,

*The Becher's Brook, one of Armscote Manor Dried Flowers'
specialities. Narrow, flat-backed arrangements such as this are ideal for
hallways and passages, where deeper arrangements might be brushed by
people passing by.*

however. Most boot rooms are terrible, pokey little corners, full of discarded footwear, muddy jackets and broken bits of pony tack, places in which dried flowers would be wasted. Something that could never be said of this boot room, and the Becher's Brook arrangement complements it entirely, managing to be both decorative and functional. Because it's such a distinctive and adaptable arrangement, I've shown how to make it in detail on page 30.

Another attractive, but practical, arrangement we put together was the design for the turn in the narrow stairs that lead from this room. It had to be an informal, country-style design – no neat baskets. We found a large copper pan that seemed to fit the stairs nicely and then chose a pretty but fairly bright selection of flowers to fill it. The material, including oats, flax, amaranthus, helichrysums, Russian statice and green honesty, was arranged quickly using chicken wire as a base, and inserted in clumps to see what the basic effect was like. As it turned out, this deceptively relaxed style gave us precisely what we were looking for.

Becher's Brook and the other arrangements we've seen all take a little time and effort to make. But for the very simplest ways of using dried flowers, I'd like to return to the kitchen. It seems to me that of all the rooms in the house, this is the place where very simple dried arrangements can be used most effectively. Formal drawing-rooms usually require something on a grand scale: bedrooms are best suited to neat, pretty designs and for the

The simplest and most informal of arrangements in an old copper pot – but even informality has to be planned before you begin work. The choice and size of container had to be right to fit this awkward turn in the stairs.

dining-table one looks for something formal and elegant. In the kitchen, however, there are opportunities for small bunches, loosely-packed baskets of hedgerow flowers and generally more informal types of presentation. But even these simple arrangements have to be used and constructed with a sense of style. All too often one sees haphazard and mismatched combinations of flowers jammed carelessly into badly-prepared containers – a few lanky grasses sticking their heads above a couple of hydrangeas, finished with a spray of sea lavender or gaudy statice protruding at an odd angle, stems displayed, and with no sense of proportion, shape or form.

You don't need exotic flowers or home-grown roses or herbs to make something look eye-catching. You don't have to spend hours making moss garlands and wiring-up bunches. With just a little style sense you can take a handful of grasses, drop them into a jug, and have an almost instant arrangement to be proud of. Naturally I'd like to encourage everyone to be more adventurous and use dried flowers in new and imaginative ways, but I also recognise the attraction of sheer simplicity. So here are my three rules for absolute no-nonsense dried-flower arrangements with a little class.

1   The paler and less interesting the contents, the more colourful and imaginative the container should be.

2   Always arrange the flowers in a smooth, rounded shape, never in a point or spikes.

3   Use enough dried material to fill the container and keep the contents in shape. Never leave gaps.

As you can see from the wonderful country kitchen shown on page 28, if you follow the guidelines you can end up with some very lovely arrangements. The attractively-shaped old basket adds form to a low-key, country-style combination of yellow achillea and quaking grass. The blue jug sets off another neatly mounded bunch of the

This kitchen has so much colour and fascinating detail to catch the eye that flowers are best kept simple. But simple doesn't have to mean boring. A strictly limited number of shades arranged in attractive containers create strong shapes which attract the attention quietly and blend harmoniously with their setting. The wooden cats, the details of the crockery and painted shutters, the flowers and the texture of the ochre-coloured walls are all shown to their full advantage.

same grass. These simple arrangements can be replaced or adapted in a matter of minutes when they become faded or dusty, or when you become bored with them. They provide a changing contrast to the equally simple but larger arrangement on the windowsill. Here a well-proportioned terracotta pot houses a beautifully-shaped arrangement of rust-coloured dudinea and verticordia. This just goes to prove that you don't have to do anything fancy to achieve a really impressive result. There are no wires, clever colour combinations or dramatic contrasts of flower forms, just a good container and a strong, uncomplicated shape.

At the top of the picture you'll see another way to create an effective and reasonably-priced display – a full hop bine, twisted around a beam, with sprays of dudinea and preserved mimosa tucked into it to add colour and warmth. If you have a suitable ceiling beam or doorframe to drape it over, a hop bine makes a dramatic addition. Hammer a few small nails into the wood and use wire to tie the bine in position.

An equally uncomplicated method was used to decorate the wonderfully-carved wall cabinet. Bunches of flowers, taken directly from the Armscote shop, were tied with raffia and suspended from each side. We chose a combination of interesting textures and colours, using both exotic and typical British species. On the left, at the top, are the bristly brown seed heads of one of the banksias, natives of Australia. Beneath it is a cloud of alchemilla and below that the pretty pink and blue seed heads of nigella. At the bottom are the silver-blue spikes of sea holly that we grow most years at Armscote. To the right, the vaguely reptilian scales of *Nervosum verticor,* a South African exotic, create an interesting focal point against the plain bunches of barley and oats. Tying and hanging the bunches was the work of a few minutes. The result? Extra colour, texture and interest that shows off the cabinet all the better.

Hanging bunches – the easiest and quickest way of decorating an isolated cupboard or dresser. And when one gets bored with the original bunches, they can be replaced by new ones with the minimum of expense and trouble.

Making the Arrangement

BECHER'S BROOK

Becher's Brook is an excellent arrangement for a beginner to attempt. It looks impressive, yet its formal construction – straight rows of flowers at different levels – means there's little chance of going wrong. Its flat-backed style makes it the ideal arrangement for setting against a wall.

The most difficult part of making a Becher's Brook is selecting the flowers. You will need a variety of tall, spiky material for the back and softer, shorter flowers for the front. Choose your colours by making sample swatches of different combinations, and don't be afraid to try out a few unlikely contrasts. For the container you need a long, narrow basket constructed of twigs. Don't worry if it has a handle as this will be hidden by the flowers. These are available from a variety of shops, from department stores to specialist florists' suppliers (see page 135). If you have difficulty in finding one, or if you wish to make a larger version of the arrangement like the one shown in our boot room picture on page 25, you can trim an ordinary woven basket with twigs or off-cut stems. Simply form the stems into small bundles and secure them vertically to the basket with U-shaped wires. When the basket is covered add a horizontal trim to hide the wires. For a more elegant variation, though not a true Becher's Brook, one could use a fish kettle or other similarly-shaped container.

MATERIALS REQUIRED
- *A long, narrow basket*
- *Dry foam blocks*
- *Stub wires*
- *Scissors and a knife*
- *A selection of flowers (in this example I used amaranthus, pink larkspur, alchemilla, roses, glixia, dahlias and hydrangeas)*

1 Cut the dry foam blocks to fit the basket. Push U-shaped wires through the basket and into the foam to hold it firmly in place. Use another U-shaped wire to hold the foam blocks together.

2 Start at the back using the tallest material. I used green amaranthus for the back row, with pink larkspur in front of it. Be careful not to place the material too close to the edge of the foam as it may break.

3 Complete one end of the arrangement so that you can work out the best proportions and how far each layer should drop below the previous one. When you are happy with this, finish the rows. Tough-stemmed material can be stuck straight into the foam, but tiny flowers or those with flexible stems will have to be wired into bunches first.

4 The flowers for the bottom row of the arrangement should be inserted so that they cover the top of the basket and conceal any glimpses of foam. Hydrangeas are ideal for the purpose.

COUNTRY HOUSE STYLE

I find country house style almost impossible to define, and yet I think most of us know what we mean when we use the phrase. For me it creates visions of eclectic collections of old furniture and treasures; traditional fabrics and colours, sometimes faded and worn; a sense of comfort and warmth, though not at the complete expense of elegance, and a feeling of continuity with the past, an ease and maturity born of time.

Flowers, of course, form an integral part of this vision and have always been an important part of country house life, both figuratively – in fabrics, papers, carvings and paintings – and literally. At Armscote I use fresh flowers in many of the rooms, but I don't always have the time to make a really exceptional feature of them. It's unfortunate, because houses like Armscote are at their best when they are full of flowers. Yet they could be, simply by introducing a few dried-flower arrangements.

I'm not going to pretend that dried flowers are a replacement for fresh ones. I believe that both should be treated very differently and valued for the specific qualities and advantages they offer. It's true that dried flowers lack the delicacy and grace of the fresh material, but it's equally true that most fresh flowers need daily attention and last for perhaps only a few days. Ideally one should use both, to ensure that whatever the season and however busy one is, there are always flowers of some kind in the house.

The lovely manor house home of my brother-in-law and his wife, Caroline, is always full of flowers. She has a bold and highly skilled sense of design and colour and for their living-room, pictured on page 33, she chose warm shades of tangerine and burnt orange. To make any kind of impact at all our arrangement had to be just as bold in colour.

The brightest highlights are supplied by the Chinese lanterns and the zinging scarlet-orange tones of the dahlias, with their ruffled petals. Orange-tufted carthamus also makes an important contribution. The light, sharp green of its foliage was a particularly good combination with the orange shades and we followed it up by choosing yellow-green alchemilla and spikes of amaranthus for contrast. To prevent the overall effect from becoming too heavy we added bunches of pale oats and quaking grass, with several shades of dyed gypsophila, some fronds of dark bracken and, for textural variation, the large, bristly heads and serrated leaves of Australian honeysuckle. Tucked in, here and there, are sprigs of dudinea and glixia in sympathetic shades. This arrangement offers a splendid splash of colour to the room when placed in a prominent position, and when there's time for fresh flowers it can be moved to a less central spot where it will brighten up a dull corner.

From the living-room we move into the dining-room. I must admit that I'm not really surprised that so many people have forsaken the formal dining-room for the cosiness of the kitchen. Grand dining-rooms are fine for special occasions, but for everyday use they're often quite impractical. And, because they're seldom used they

A classic basket arrangement of brilliant orange dahlias and Chinese lanterns makes a warming contribution to a living-room. Dahlias are quite unusual and much nicer, I think, dried than fresh. For a little exotic texture we added a couple of bristly Australian banksias with their distinctive serrated leaves near the base of the arrangement.

tend to have a rather chilly and unlived-in feel when the time does come to get out the monogrammed silver and the crystal. Anything one can do to add colour helps, and one sure way is to use dried flowers. They can be left, untended, during those periods when the room is unused, and will look fine on their own for Sunday lunches or informal occasions. For something more grand try combining them with fresh flowers for a really full effect.

Not all dining-rooms are chilly and unlived in, of course. In fact chilly is the very last word one might use to describe the one pictured here. It is warm, welcoming and just one of many bold, beautiful and comfortable rooms in a quite glorious manor house not far from Banbury in Oxfordshire. I'm fortunate enough to have been a guest here, and it really is the most remarkable place for a dinner party.

When it came to designing a dried-flower arrangement for such a setting, our first challenge was to attempt to define the colour of the panelling and walls. A sort of maroon, we agreed at first. Then the sun came out and opinions were divided. Brick red and rust red were volunteered for the main colour of the walls, and a crimson red suggested for some of the details. We realized that there was going to be very little chance of matching the colour and that it was best not to try.

A bold, beautiful dining-room.
When you are designing
flowers for a room decorated
in a strong and subtle colour,
like this one, it's easier and often
more effective to look for contrasts
than to try and match shades.
The basket in the fireplace is a
good example of how this can
work spectacularly well. The
strong blues, pinks and green
bring out the best from the rusty-
red walls.

It was a wise decision and one which I would advocate to anyone else facing a similar problem. Materials that match a room's colour scheme can give you initial confidence when starting an arrangement, but if you get too obsessed with colour co-ordination the end result can be flowers that echo their background so closely that they almost disappear. The nearest match we found for this room was red capucin leaves, a few of which can be seen in the basket in the fireplace. Unfortunately when we tried using them in the smaller arrangements they had a rather depressing effect and had to be removed. Faced with this there was no alternative but to look for contrasts. We decided, after a few experiments, to pick up the secondary colour of the curtains, blue, and strong violet-pink. The results were certainly not boring.

Many of us own attractive glass and silverware that is rarely used and seldom seen. I like the idea of putting these items to use in the dining-room, where they seem most at home. Better to have them full of dried flowers than gathering dust or looking empty and forlorn on the side-table. By the fireplace is a glass bon-bon dish containing a simple arrangement that includes green amaranthus, pink roses and peonies, blue larkspur and the distinctive soft red of leptospermum, commonly known as silver strawberry.

When making an arrangement in a glass container, it's advisable to line it first so that the plastic foam, wires and other fixings are invisible from the outside. This isn't always necessary if one is using cut glass because the patterns obscure the contents, but I always think it's worth doing anyway. For the bon-bon dish we used potpourri, which had the added advantage of perfuming the room. One can just as easily use moss, leaves, lavender or flat flower heads. To fix the foam inside the container we used strips of florists' tape (see page 134). As I have said before, this is the only method I would suggest if you're using cut

glass or any other precious container that mustn't be marked or scratched.

The low arrangements on the table were made in two silver dishes, which were first lined with thick black polythene to prevent scratches from the wires. Again, the foam was held firmly in place with a few strips of florists' tape stretched across the top. The flowers include lavender, nigella, pale pink peonies, pink dudinea and flax, which has tiny, nodding, ball-shaped heads with subtle touches of pink and purple. It's a robust and interesting way of softening an arrangement, much better than sea lavender or gypsophila. The dishes were finished with pieces of sphagnum moss tucked around the edges to hide any glimpses of foam that might have been reflected by the shiny table.

For the centrepiece we used a delicate silver epergne with four glass flutes. It's the ideal container for this situation, with enough height and character to attract attention, yet not so tall and bulky that it dominates the table and blocks the view of the diners. I greatly appreciate the opportunity of using antique pieces like this, which might otherwise have spent most of their lives hidden in the back of a cupboard. If they are filled with dried flowers you can keep them proudly on display, knowing they are making a positive contribution to the setting.

Each of the epergne's glass flutes was lined with potpourri and filled with small pieces of plastic foam, then arranged with the same selection of flowers that were used in the low dishes. These arrangements are simple rounded shapes, easy enough for even a beginner to tackle and very quick to complete. Rather more demanding and time-consuming is the large basket in the hearth, which uses the same colours and flowers as the table arrangements but includes a few extra additions, such as sharp-green amaranthus and rusty-red capucin leaves. I think it helps to have one large design like this in a room where there are a number of smaller arrangements. On their own the smaller arrangements may look bitty and lost, but if they are seen in conjunction with larger features they become part of an integrated scheme.

Other ideas for decorating a formal dinner-table might include a wide, flower-filled garland that runs the length of the table. Use large flowers such as hydrangeas, delphiniums, peonies and celosia to bulk it out, with mimosa and glycerined ivy (see page 131) to trail attractively across the table.

For a luxurious talking point, why not wire some beautiful fruit into the garland? Mouthwatering purple figs and blue-black grapes, trailing brambles covered in blackberries, the glossy autumn colours of pomegranates, pinkish lychees, bright orange kumquats and wrinkled passion fruit – they would all look superb. For a variation on the same theme, make individual arrangements of dried flowers and fruit in small bowls or terracotta pots and use one to decorate each place setting. At the end of the meal guests can be invited to help themselves to fruit from the arrangements.

The setting for the next two photographs, shown on pages 38-9 and 40, is one of the most idyllic of all the houses you'll see in this book. It belongs to a family friend, Jane Brabyn, who is the granddaughter of Sir Thomas Beecham and is herself a fine musician. She also has interesting and serious views about the conservation of old houses such as her own. Her policy is to repair when necessary, but not to renovate unduly, to allow the passage of time to show in the fabric of the buildings and to live with the character of her home, rather than trying to change it. Her sympathetic approach is one that conservationists are adopting in ever-increasing numbers in Great Britain and perhaps explains why this manor house

has such a tranquil atmosphere.

Designing dried flowers for such an individual home was a challenge. Rigid forms, overtly fashionable shapes and self-consciously clever designs were out. So were bright colours, which would have looked new and harsh. Nothing too simple was in order because these rooms are large and formal, yet neither was anything that was excessively smart or showy. Sometimes when you walk into a room it is immediately obvious what kind of arrangement is required. If it's not, I try to find inspiration from the fabrics, furniture and objects displayed in the room. Usually something will spark off an idea or a theme that I can use. In this case three things made an impression. First, the warm brown colours of the wooden floor and the bookcase. Second, the mosaic of colours and patterns in the rugs. And third, the colours and textures of the velvet curtains (not, sadly, visible in the picture) and the upholstery of the chair.

For the rug-draped ottoman we chose a large, traditional basket arrangement composed of clear, harmonious reds, yellows and oranges to give a warm but not too vivid

One classic arrangement and one work of imagination, both inspired by the colours, textiles and patterns of this lovely room and both successful on their own terms

effect. The colour comes predominently from red and yellow roses and orange verticordia, but a closer look will reveal that it is studded with other colours. Pink heather, white gypsophila, blue hydrangeas and pale blue delphiniums and larkspur are just a few of the varieties mingled in with the green ferns. The effect is rather like that of the rugs, which are full of colours that one doesn't notice at first glance.

On the table by the windowsill we made a very free arrangement which is based round the extraordinary colours and textures of celosia, which looks like crushed velvet. In feel and appearance it is quite unlike any other kind of dried flower. I am normally fairly careful about the way I use this plant because there can be something almost too rich and opulent about it. In small quantities it is extremely useful for adding depth of colour and textural contrast to an arrangement, and it goes well in traditionally-styled Victorian settings full of velvet and moquette. It works here, I think, because it is tempered by the plainness of the surrounding foliage and the lack of pattern and strong colour in its immediate vicinity.

This is the kind of imaginative arrangement for which there are few guidelines. In fact almost the only thing I can recommend to those embarking on something totally original, like this, is to make it bold and not to stint

The strong shape and overwhelming darkness of this grand piano demands an arrangement with plenty of character – supplied here by a carved wooden statue surrounded by a thicket of wild-looking flowers and foliage. To the right of it, in complete contrast, is the only traditional triangular-shaped arrangement you'll find in this book. It's pretty, and still popular with people who like their flowers neat and tidy.

on materials. Apart from that, one simply has to trust one's own judgement. Personally, I believe it's worked here, and so did Jane Brabyn, who was appreciative of its free and full shape and liked the fact that it was so different from other, less creative, arrangements.

When it came to arrangements for the main hall of the manor with its huge stone fireplace and grand piano, it took us some time to work out what was needed. The piano is a wonderful feature, but because of its size and colour it tends to dominate the picture. Something was required to go on top of it, but a basket arrangement just wouldn't do. We needed something with more height and impact – but what? When, after some time, we'd come up with neither a container we felt was right for the setting, nor any ideas for an arrangement, we decided to try a different approach. We chose an object that had the right kind of height and impact, and decorated that.

If you ever find yourself in a similar state of creative paralysis, you might find this a useful way of freeing yourself. Forget your hidebound ideas of what makes a traditional arrangement and look around for other sources of inspiration.

One idea was sparked off by the number of musical instruments around the house. Many of them belong to Jane's partner Michael Tubbs, who is Music Director of the Royal Shakespeare Company and a brilliant musician. We contemplated making an arrangement incorporating a violin and bow, a flute, a roll of musical manuscript and any other musical bits and pieces we could gather. What we had in mind was a very stylized arrangement alluding to the woodcarvings of Grinling Gibbons, many of which included flowers. The idea had to be abandoned when we discovered that no one would lend us their precious flutes and violins, but it is something that I'd like to try in future.

A second suggestion was to use a classically shaped candelabra and add flowers to that. This was rejected, however, because it seemed rather clichéd, but I'm sure it would have looked good.

Our eventual solution was to base the arrangement around a wooden figure we have at Armscote. This is a carving of the Wandering Jew, Ahasuerus by name, which I bought at an auction some years ago. I remember the occasion particularly well because it was just after Fred and I were married and I'd gone to London with the intention of buying some furniture for our first home. I returned to the Cotswolds with nothing to show for the trip except the wooden statue. Fred was not impressed. I'm delighted, however, that after all this time my purchase has proved itself so useful!

The flowers had to be dramatic to stand out against the large scale of the piano and also to match the strong (some have even said malevolent) character of Ahasuerus. We developed a dense mass of multi-textured and coloured foliage from which the figure emerges. A branch cut from a smoke tree and preserved in glycerine provides the vertical element of a tall, curved shape that exploits the turning movement of the figure. Twigs covered in silver lichen, pink titree, tall sprays of yellow kangaroo paw and spiky grey-topped *Phylica rigida* give way to weeping pear, mahonia, ferns and beech arranged in a tightly-packed bunch. At the rear of the arrangement twisted banana branches add to the drama, suggesting the broken and twisted roots of an old tree. Glycerined ivy trails over the statue's arm and down on to the piano. Further strands tumble over the edges. The finishing touch is a bird's nest complete with eggs, half-hidden amidst the foliage and positioned so that it's the focus of Ahasuerus' wild gaze. This is not a traditionally 'pretty' arrangement, but a strong, dramatic creation that reflects its setting.

*The two splendid ducks, the wildlife embroideries standing behind them
and the watercolour on the wall behind the arrangement were our
inspiration for this moss-covered riverbank design. Children in
particular love this type of arrangement as they can keep adding things
to the miniature landscape.*

This is a good point at which to add a few words about the use of dried flowers on pianos. Vases of fresh flowers are usually banned from pianos because of the potential water damage to the wood and, disaster, the inner workings. With dried flowers there is no such danger. Furthermore, depending, of course, on the container, dried arrangements also have the advantage of being lighter than water-filled ones. This makes them particularly suitable for old and delicate pieces of furniture, radiator screens and for high shelves, where it would be difficult to keep lifting a heavy fresh arrangement up and down. I don't particularly wish to promote dried flowers for their practical advantages – they should stand by their looks alone – but they can, without doubt, be very useful additions to the interior design repertoire.

On now to two arrangements designed specifically to suit a particular item of furniture. The first, pictured on page 43, is a chest of drawers. When we saw the setting, with the ducks and the watercolours hanging on the wall, nothing came immediately to mind. We considered making a garlanded basket filled with pomanders, or a large, low basket full of russet-coloured flowers, but neither seemed entirely suitable. A glass bowl lined with moss and filled with pine cones, acorns, seed heads and flowers was more appealing, except that a plain glass bowl didn't seem to be totally in keeping with the setting. We at last realized that the work had already been done for us by the owner of the house. Our keys were the ducks and the watercolours depicting a peaceful country scene.

An arrangement fills the difficult gap left above a wardrobe perfectly. The shape, size and contents of the design were all planned and sketched beforehand so that we could judge the proportions.

The resulting arrangement is based on the idea of a riverbank. We filled a basket with off cuts of dry foam and covered it in different mosses – mounded green bun moss to create smooth rounded shapes, touches of lichen and greyish Spanish moss around the sides for texture and colour. We then looked for a variety of other materials that would be appropriate in this miniature landscape. Caustus, glycerined ivy, dried fungi, spiky skeletal agapanthus heads and small bell-shaped eucalyptus seeds were all wired into position. Interesting stones were brought in from the garden and glued into the arrangement. The final touches were the six bulrushes pushed firmly into the moss at the back.

A miniature landscape like this can be great fun, especially for children who love to keep adding things. I think you have to treat this kind of arrangement with a little humour, but because in this case the whole context – the slightly whimsical ducks (particularly the one on the left, which has a very peculiar look in its eye), the embroidery and the painting – was right, the arrangement fitted perfectly.

Our second design or 'set piece' was for the top of a wonderful old painted wardrobe, shown opposite, that formed a major feature in a spacious drawing-room. The problem with even the most beautiful wardrobes is that they tend to stop abruptly a foot or two from the ceiling, leaving a difficult and not always very attractive space. The owner of this particular piece of furniture often uses fresh material to fill the gap, but one can imagine the inconvenience of climbing up there with water-filled containers. Dried flowers were the obvious alternative.

Taking as a source of inspiration the nuts and flowers painted on the wardrobe itself, our first thought was to create an arrangement using oak leaves and acorns, nuts, fir cones and red flowers to add a touch of bright colour. By the time we had gathered a swatch of colours and materials, however, we realized that this was going to look too heavy and dark. Something lighter, both in texture and colour, was required. We began again with a new swatch and chose strong, sunny yellows as our main shade. When it came to selecting materials we looked for those with a strong, distinctive form that could be appreciated from ground level. The use of intricate textures and details is marvellous if they can be seen, but in an arrangement such as this, the detail would be lost so it is best to stick with strong simple forms.

Our final selection included the drumstick-shaped flowers of craspedia, kangaroo paw and yellow roses. Those invaluable fillers, carthamus, alchemilla and amaranthus supplied most of the greenery, while dark brown bracken gave the whole arrangement depth and solidity. Tucked in amongst the other material to give an occasional touch of more complex colour were a few rust-brown and orange flowers. Do try this yourself when you are making arrangements that are predominantly one shade. Just a few flowers of a different colour added so unobtrusively that the eye doesn't consciously see them can bring the whole arrangement to life.

Our materials were arranged in a low, mounded shape that trailed over the edge of the wardrobe. This was done purposely to break-up the heavy top line of the piece. Without the fronds of bracken and kangaroo paw intruding over the edge, it would have looked as if our flowers were just sitting on the top – a decorative afterthought, but not an integral part of the picture.

I find it very useful when designing an arrangement like this to use a pencil and paper to sketch the setting and see how the design will look in context. Measure all the relevant fittings and items of furniture so that you can work out how tall or broad the arrangement needs to be.

Upstairs, now, to two bedrooms that couldn't be more different in design and atmosphere. While we were looking for our locations and planning the arrangements, we discussed the kind of dried flowers we had encountered in bedrooms in the past and were astonished to discover that everyone seemed to have a horror story to tell – of hotel bedrooms with bunches of pampas grass shedding all over the carpet, of elderly aunts whose spare rooms housed hideous, dusty bulrushes, and holiday apartments with sparse, fluff-covered arrangements of statice beside each bed. It was a salutory experience.

Pampas grass and bulrushes certainly don't feature in our bedrooms, but I readily accept the point about dust. All dried flowers require occasional dusting, but it is particularly important in the bedroom, especially if one has an arrangement by the bed. Dust them regularly, using a large, soft paintbrush or a hair dryer on a low setting. One can also obtain a miniature vacuum device sold for cleaning computer keyboards and other inaccessible crevices. If you're using one of these, try it out at the back of the arrangement first, just in case it removes the flowers along with the dust.

Our first bedroom, shown on page 47, is traditionally pretty, decorated in soft colours and flowery fabrics. Something simple seemed in order and so we filled an attractively-shaped terracotta bowl with a low arrange-

Though this is a sophisticated bedroom, the exposed beams add a pleasing hint of rusticity. It's this contrast we wanted to echo in the bedside arrangement. A rustic terracotta bowl is complemented by a pretty, but pleasingly restrained, garden arrangement of roses, nigella and alchemilla. And surrounding it is a terracotta dish filled with potpourri.

ment of pink and crimson flowers. They include hel-ichrysums, alchemilla, pink and white larkspur, roses, crimson-dyed quaking grass and nigella. The result is attractive enough to stand on its own, but we wanted to make it a little more special. Two ideas came to mind. One was to put the bowl in a larger terracotta saucer and fill the gap around it with more dried flowers. In the end, though, we decided to place the bowl at an angle to show off the flowers better, and filled the saucer with potpourri and pieces of broken pottery.

Potpourri is one of the oldest and most delightful ways of scenting a room and has been used in country houses since the Middle Ages. Used as part of an arrange-ment like this, it is pleasing to both the nose and the eye. We chose to use a traditional rose-based mixture to com-plement the flowers in the arrangement, but there are many other types of scent and mood to choose from. For something deeper and more spicy, try one based on heather or lavender with cinnamon and cloves. Citrus pot-pourri, containing dried orange and lemon peel, is tangy and refreshing, good for bathrooms, while for a man's dressing-room or study one might choose a mixture with overtones of cedar and sandalwood. One could even use potpourri as inspiration for a dried-flower arrangement. It would be fun, for example, to decorate a basket of spiced lavender mixture with a garland containing some lavender flowers, cinnamon sticks and pomanders stuck with cloves.

For the dressing-table, outlined against the mul-lioned stone window, we chose three small arrangements. On the left is a tree covered in the same combination of flowers we used in the bedside arrangement. If one is making a variety of arrangements for the same room it is generally wise to include some of the same materials in the arrangements, thus creating a link and a sense of con-tinuity. This doesn't mean that the same flowers *have* to be used throughout. An occasional colour or textural contrast throws a new perspective on all the arrangements and can make them even more interesting.

Making a small tree like the one on the dressing-table is a relatively easy task. Instructions for setting the trunk in plaster are on page 69. A dry foam shape can be attached to the trunk once it has firmly set. Spheres and cones are commercially available from florists (see page 135) or you can carve your own irregular shape from a larger block. The next stage is to decide the effect you're aiming for and to choose your flowers accordingly. Celo-sia, used on its own, gives a wonderfully rich, velvety re-sult. Helichrysums stuck densely all over can give a very full, mop-headed, effect. A plain green moss tree looks marvellously simple, particularly if it has an interesting, gnarled trunk. Alternatively if you cover a cone with dark green spikes of kunzea then you have a Christmas tree. Arrange a number of twigs together in the plaster and top them with greenery and you have a bonsai-sized copse. The possibilities are simply endless, limited only by the imagination.

In our case, we wrapped the tree's trunk in larkspur stalks to give it a more interesting texture and followed the contours of the sphere fairly closely when adding the flowers. The whole arrangement is finished off with bun moss piled around the base.

Next to it is a very simple, lace-edged posy, made to a formal design in a commercially available posy holder (see page 134). To the right, echoing the contents of the bed-side arrangement, is a small basket of potpourri finished with a garland, another fragrant touch to a very feminine corner of the room.

There's not a posy or rosebud to be seen in our second bedroom pictured on pages 50-51. Situated in the attic of a

For this traditionally pretty bedrom we chose small, neat arrangements.
The tree, posy and garlanded basket full of potpourri are ideal
attractive but unobtrusive additions to the dressing-table displaying
family photos.

A fantasy bedroom. The sparse, romantic feel of the room is reflected in the arrangements. In the foreground, contorted willow branches create dramatic, visually exciting shapes. At the back, a bundle of reeds tied in a basic sheaf makes the simplest and least fussy of arrangements.

fascinating old house that stands on its own in a gloriously rolling Cotswold valley not far from Northleach, it's a fantasy creation – a room for a romantic individualist with a strongly dramatic streak. The house itself is a mysterious place, the remaining wing of what must once have been a country residence built on a grand and imposing scale. It's said to be haunted by two ghosts, one of whom makes occasional appearances in the attic. I have to report that we saw nothing of it while we were there, but the atmosphere of the place certainly influenced our choice of arrangements.

The sparse, fantastic feel of the room was perplexing at first after the comfortable, colourful interiors we were used to. What kind of arrangements could adequately reflect the attic's character? Country baskets and traditionally pretty garlands were out. They were too sturdy, too solid and, anyway, not large enough to make much impact. What was needed in this environment were designs with an ethereal quality; sparse, fantastical arrangements that

relied on architectural rather than decorative impact.

Back at Armscote we began to collect materials and colour samples, and found ourselves reaching automatically for light, cool colours – blues, greys, whites, silvers – and materials with an airy feel or strong form. It was a disconcerting experience. Where were the reds and oranges normally used to provide warmth? Where were the bunches of green foliage to act as fillers? We understood instinctively that we wanted to do something different, but avoiding established ways of thinking proved difficult at times.

The material that really inspired us and provided the key for the other arrangements was a bundle of contorted willow bought from New Covent Garden market in London (see page 135). This is wonderful stuff, with branches that naturally twist into tortured shapes. It is often cut, stripped of its leaves and added to flower arrangements to give instant movement and drama. As soon as we snipped the strings that bound our bundle together and watched the branches splay out into their contorted, windblown shapes, we knew we had our first arrangement. The willow was fixed in an old churn and finished with a bunch of silvery-white seacrest. The result was scarcely typical country house style, but was exactly suited to its location.

The other large arrangement standing against the back wall is equally simple and yet it was a real discovery. We came across it by accident during a trip to the Royal Show at Stoneleigh in Warwickshire, where almost every facet of farming and country life is represented in displays, competitions and exhibits. Among those demonstrating their country crafts were a group of thatchers who, as well as explaining the finer points of their art, showed us samples of the different reeds that were available to them. We came away with a bundle of the longest reeds they had, tied them into a sheaf, and for less than two pounds achieved an arrangement of extraordinary simplicity and dramatic impact.

In a romantic gesture we cast practicality to the wind and hung a swing from the central roof beam. As the heavy nylon ropes were rather less romantic than desired, we covered them in grey Spanish moss, which was then trimmed with delphiniums, white *Helichrysum vestitum capblumen*, known as vestitum, and blue-dyed glixia. For the pelmet across the doorway and the curtain tie-back we used a narrow garland wired with sea lavender, gypsophila, dark blue delphiniums and statice, glixia and more of the white daisies. Informal bunches of statice and delphiniums, with alchemilla, poppy heads, bleached grasses and nigella added extra colour and texture tucked into an enamel jug and hung from the bedpost. Behind the bed an old tin hatbox was filled with spiky delphiniums and white larkspur, with the button-shaped heads of botao and sprays of oats and sea lavender. The overall effect is almost surreal. It's a place of the imagination, of fantasy – perhaps even of ghosts.

One wouldn't normally put flowers on a sunny windowsill because the light makes them fade quickly, but as this was a fantasy room free from the constraints of practicality we chose to bend the rules. We found an old fireplace fender that matched the size of the heavy beam running under the window and filled it with a long row of flowers. The same materials were used as elsewhere in the room, with the botao 'buttons' providing a central focal point. Our search for materials turned up an anonymous bundle of fine, wispy reeds, which we inserted in clumps to give the arrangement height and found they added a rather mysterious feel. The lower, stubbier clumps are bunches of glixia stems, cut off when the glixia were wired and re-used here. There can be a great deal of wastage in dried-

A windowsill detail. Working with sharp, 'difficult' colours can be a rewarding experience. Too often we play safe with pretty, inoffensive colours that give us bland results. As long as an arrangement works in context, as this one does, it really doesn't matter whether it's pretty or not.

flower arranging, especially if one is wiring-up small bunches of flowers to insert in larger arrangements for a pleasingly full effect. I like to find interesting ways of re-cycling some of the discarded stalks and foliage, as here, for example, or to cover baskets or miniature tree trunks.

Our interest in dramatic form and shape inspired one last arrangement, which we used to top a makeshift book-case constructed from an old stepladder. The overall height and shape was provided by silver tentacles of sea-crest, this time juxtaposed with the wonderful spiky shapes of globe thistles. All the materials were arranged in a tall glass tank lined with silver-blue lavender potpourri.

This lining technique is not difficult but can take time to achieve a pleasing result. Start by measuring the dimensions of the container and cutting a piece of dry foam to go inside, leaving a gap of between a quarter and half an inch (0.6-1.2cm) all round. Pour some of the lining mat-erial into the bottom of the container, insert the foam and hold in position while you pour lavender or potpourri

around it. If you have someone available to help, ask them to hold the foam and container. You can then try roll-ing-up a sheet of paper to make a narrow funnel and pour-ing the lavender through this, directly into position. The results vary dramatically according to the material you use for the lining. A rose-based potpourri gives a very dark, rich texture. Lavender is glistening and cool whilst cinna-mon sticks poked down between the glass and foam give a stripy, woody texture. Different types of moss and lichen, used together or separately, create a variety of patterns.

Too often people's conception of dried flowers is limited to basket arrangements and vases filled with dusty, long dead material. But that very same material can become high art when used with a little imagination. What I hope we've demonstrated in this attic is that dried flowers can be as dramatic and as visually exciting as you dare to make them. Whatever the mood or effect you want to achieve in your home, there are dried materials and tech-niques that can realize your vision.

An exercise in form, with tentacles of seacrest making a wonderful contrast to the prickly spheres of the globe thistles. Too often, as flower arrangers, we wire and trim our material into the shapes we require for traditional, unimaginative arrangements. It's a liberation, once in a while, to look at the same material from a new perspective; to see not just its colour but its natural shape and form, and to use those natural qualities in an arrangement.

TOWN MEETS COUNTRY

Traditional manor houses like those featured in this book, most of them built in the sixteenth and seventeenth centuries, have a special charm that appeals to people the world over. They are, for many, the classic embodiment of the smaller English country house. But it would be a mistake to forget all the other beautiful houses of later centuries – particularly those Georgian and early Victorian houses that make such wonderful country homes. The style and character of such houses is quite different from the old manors. Later architecture followed new lines that were a self-conscious move away from the low ceilings and dim interiors of the older houses. If traditional manors were characterized by the huge stone hearths and wooden beams dominating their rooms, those houses of the eighteenth and nineteenth centuries offered large windows, high ceilings and detailed decoration.

The change in style was influenced not just by architectural fashion, but by a deeper social change that drew people away from the country to live in the city. The poor went to cities to find work. The rich went to enjoy themselves. (Anyone who is familiar with the novels of Jane Austen will remember how many of her characters longed to escape from the boredom of the countryside for the bright lights and adventure of Bath and London.) A landowner visiting his country estate wanted a house in which he could enjoy some of the comforts and sophistications he'd learned to appreciate in town. And so we get beautiful Georgian and, later, Victorian houses – houses that bring a touch of the city to the countryside.

When we visited houses like this, we realized that our dried-flower arrangements would need to reflect their sophisticated character without becoming too formal. Our first challenge was the vast, soft-white painted reception-room pictured on page 57 with its impressive marble fireplace and detailed plasterwork panels, typical of many a town house. The room could have been very grand, but instead it has been furnished with sofas and chairs in traditional chintzes that give it a comfortable and lived-in feel. The white walls and plain wooden floor, scattered with old rugs, have a clean, modern look. We decided to combine the two, modern and traditional, for a series of arrangements on the mantlepiece.

The clear, pretty colours of the chintz set the colours of our arrangements, and for containers we chose a variety of styles, new and old. We began with the new. Two tall glass vases were lined with a mixture of lavender and rose petals and filled with rich, unashamedly pretty arrangements of pink roses, larkspur and titree, with green amaranthus and the spidery seed heads of *Nigella orientalis*, a new and very attractive introduction. Touches of strong blue-green glixia added a note of contrast – a necessity if the arrangements weren't to look too cloyingly pretty. The tops of the vases were covered with plaited paper ribbon for a neat and distinctive look.

For the other arrangements we used some of the owner's cachepots and filled each of them with different combinations of flowers in the same colour theme. To the one on the left were added bright pink clumps of silene,

Variations on a theme inspired by chintz. New glass vases and old porcelain cachepots make compatible companions on this imposing mantlepiece. When you are grouping arrangements together like this, use an uneven number. Three or five arrangements always look better than two or four.

soft yellow verticordia, apricot-coloured statice, hydrangeas, dyed gypsophila, helichrysums and wonderfully full-blown peonies. The pot in the centre is packed with small bunches of different coloured glixia, which together give a dappled light-and-shade effect. On the right-hand side there are more roses and *Nigella orientalis*, arranged with botao heads and the tiny bead-like heads of flax. Glixia and alchemilla add areas of sharper colour. Five arrangements on a single mantelpiece may seem extravagant, but the best way of using dried flowers for a really bold statement is to do so lavishly. Incidentally, when grouping arrangements together always use an odd number, never even. For some reason an odd number of items, whatever they are, always looks better than two, or four or other even combinations.

In the fireplace below is the kind of arrangement that everyone with an open fire should have. It's by far the most attractive way of filling a hearth in the summer months, when blazing log fires are out of fashion. No more yawning black holes in the wall or unseasonal piles of pine cones thrown hastily into the grate. Suddenly, the fireplace becomes the focal point of the room, as it is supposed to be. The peonies are particularly spectacular in this arrangement. Their large, distinctively-textured flowers really stand out from this angle. It's helpful when you're making an arrangement that will go on the floor, like this one, to put it down occasionally and check it from the angle at which it will be viewed. Insert the strongest, most dramatic flowers and materials where they will have the maximum impact – which is not necessarily where you would imagine it to be if you are working on a table.

To achieve the required height and span in this kind of arrangement, fill the top of the container with scrunched chicken wire pulled roughly into the shape you're aiming for – in this case a tall mound, flat at the back and sloping gradually down at the front. There's something of a mystique about using chicken wire, and it's quite unfounded. Most people find that once they have mastered the skill they prefer it to dry foam. To start, take a piece of one and a half inch (3cm) gauge wire (see page 134), that's six inches (15cm) or so bigger all round than the top of the container – allow for more if it's particularly large or if you want to make a shape that rises above it. Taking each edge in turn, loosely tuck them under by two or three inches (5-7.5cm). Do this once more and then fit the resulting mass of wire into the container. It should fit firmly. If it feels loose, remove it and pull it out a little. Fix it in place with wires threaded through the basket weave or with florists' tape (see page 134). Now all you have to do is cut the flowers to length and push them into place. If the chicken wire has been properly prepared the various layers will catch the stems and hold them securely. It's a technique suitable for most types of containers and all sorts of arrangements. The three cachepots on the mantelpiece, for example, were all arranged with chicken wire.

Chicken wire is the underpinning, too, of the beautiful wall wreath featured opposite. When we first discussed ideas for some kind of arrangement to go on the wall, we had dim memories of flowery ceramic wall plaques of the 1920s and 30s. Their strong relief and irregular gaps and contours were our initial inspiration, though the finished article bears little resemblance to the original – which is as it should be. Concrete references and ideas should be the springboards for inspiration, nothing more.

For the basic shape of our dried-flower wall plaque we used a child's plastic hula-hoop and covered it in thick layers of moss and chicken wire to create a flat, irregular wreath. Two thick twigs were placed across the gap, mossed and wired into place. The basic structure com-

*Wall flowers. Wreath arrangements offer really creative opportunities if
you don't limit yourself to symmetrical shapes and designs. Make your
own irregular bases and experiment with colour in your arrangement,
starting with light shades and progressing to the darkest you can find.
Use flowers for painterly effects, as shown here, or play with texture in
a dramatic way. See, for example, how effectively button-shaped botao
heads have been grouped to create a strong, suede-textured area.*

A small tree takes up the chintz theme, its pot embedded in a basket of mind-your-own-business plants (Soleirolia soleirolii). *On the wall beside it a wonderfully textured and coloured wreath shows off massed salmon pink roses and the delicate frilled petals of peonies.*

plete, the background material – alchemilla, dyed broom bloom, yellow verticordia, flax, amaranthus and pink larkspur – was added. Over this background went the roses, peonies, hydrangeas, lavender bunches and botao buttons, all arranged in strong groups of concentrated colour and texture that made a real feature of their individual qualities. To open the roses and show them at their best, each was gently steamed over a kettle for a few seconds until it softened enough for its petals to be teased apart. The peonies were steamed and opened in the same way. The result of all this attention was an arrangement quite unlike anything seen before, a truly original design, full of beautiful flowers.

The Indian feel of the inlaid chest of drawers, shown on page 61, inspired another highly original design. We wanted to exploit the Indian theme and so as a starting point we made a list of the associations India has for us: these included rice, cotton, coconuts, cinnamon and a range of other more exotic spices. We then began collecting these and other materials that could be useful, not limiting ourselves too strictly to Indian plants and produce. A trip to the delicatessen produced licorice sticks, almonds, tamarinds in their brown, warty pods, knobbly pieces of dried root ginger and dried tomatoes. The brown and cream colour scheme, echoing that of the chest itself, was already beginning to emerge.

Elsewhere we gathered lotus seed pods, exotic-- looking seed heads, dark spires of dock, 'brown eyes' daisies, poppadums, nutmegs, bamboo sticks, vanilla pods. Attempts to find dried cotton, rice and even tea failed, but by then we had enough material for our arrangement. The result, as you can see, is dramatically original and works well with the chest of drawers that inspired it. On a purely practical note, when you're using fruit, nuts or anything that might leak or become sticky (the coconuts, for

*An Indian-inspired arrangement, witty and sophisticated, packed with
intriguing and unusual contents, including lotus pods, poppadums,
nutmegs, bamboo sticks and vanilla pods. It is dramatically original
and perfect for its setting.*

example) in an arrangement, line the container with plastic so that no damage is done to the furniture.

Of course there are many other types of arrangement that could have worked well in this position. A simple basket filled with flowers in shades of yellow, brown and green would have looked pleasing, though perhaps rather dull. On a more adventurous note, an arrangement with mother-of-pearl shells, like those used for the chest inlay, could have been visually exciting – although perhaps a little gaudy for this calm setting. Maybe, taking into account the seascape on the wall, an arrangement based on an interesting piece of driftwood would have been appropriate. Not all settings inspire this number of options, but by simply looking for associations one is usually agreeably surprised by the ideas that emerge.

Another bold arrangement in its use of exotic material, shown opposite, was created for a difficult corner of a living-room. It was difficult because of the busy background of the quilt and the strong shape of the painted wooden horse that was already standing in front of it. Despite the fact that both horse and quilt have a rustic look, together they create a sophisticated visual combination. Any arrangement that was to complement them had to be equally commanding. A country basket simply wasn't going to be enough.

As starting points we took the strong brown and red colours in the horse's saddle and the spiky triangular motifs of the quilt. Fortunately the ideal container, a red and black water carrier bought on a holiday in Thailand, was soon found and the search for materials began. Spiky palm spears and the strongly serrated leaves and bristly heads of *Banksia baxteri* were obvious choices for their form. Vibrant red verticordia and celosia, brown-dyed broom bloom and reddish-brown capucin leaves joined the pile. So did the grey, fluffy textures of *Phylica rigida*,

dark red helichrysums, proteas, some dramatic brown seed pods and the cream-coloured spikes of dryandra. Dusty, blue-black, preserved palm berries were piled into the lid of the water carrier, which was set down in front of the arrangement. The result was about as far from a traditional country house style as one could possibly get, wildly exotic, highly dramatic, and absolutely right for this particular location.

There is a kind of flair and boldness about this arrangement which I associate with the European school of floristry. The Dutch and Germans lead the way in continental flower design, and their ideas and arrangements are often strikingly different from English style. So many English florists and gardeners, myself included, love the idea of informality, wildflowers, cottage gardens, simple arrangements – in short, the natural look. The Dutch and Germans do not share our near-obsession with nature. They love bright, dyed colours, artificial shapes and exotic material used in fantastic ways – a kind of floral modernism that leaves most English observers in a state of shock.

I have an example of this type of modern, continental arrangement at Armscote and sometimes use it to surprise visitors who ask me about fashions in dried flowers. It was made for me by a wonderful young Dutch designer who came to Armscote two or three years ago to help develop

Exotic flowers and spiky textures mingle in this bold, brave arrangement with more than a dash of continental flair. Fearful English florists might quail at the thought of grouping banksias, palm spears and proteas in front of this rustic-looking setting, but a touch of drama is exactly what the grouping requires. It's a lesson to all of us, myself, I admit, included, in how to use exotic materials with style.

some new ideas for our range. At the end of her time with us, during which she produced lots of wonderful arrangements, I suggested she let herself go and make something more creative in her own favourite style. The result was a white plastic bowl filled with metallic florentine branches, corn cobs, gypsophila and glixia, much of it sprayed with pale green metallic paint. Bleached *Briza segromi*, she told us, represented the female and the corn cobs the male – and we had no problem at all in understanding the symbolism. When I show it to English guests and ask their opinion there is a silence followed by a gulp and a strangled, 'Well, it's . . . interesting.' Not a very flattering response.

It's not, fortunately, difficult to find something flattering to say about the pair of daisy trees that flank the garden door in the picture on the right. In season a pair of real daisy trees occupy this position, but at other times of the year these dried-flower lookalikes replace them. You need a large-scale setting and plenty of confidence to carry off arrangements this size, but if you have both then the effect can be quite spectacular. Large trees are at their best when they are used symmetrically in pairs (this is the one exception to the odd numbers rule cited on page 58), as they are here. They'd look good standing either side of a fireplace or at the base of an imposing staircase.

When one is making a major statement with arrangements such as these, I would advise a fairly conservative choice of colours and materials. Bright, clashy shades are fun for small trees, but used in something larger and more attention-grabbing they may soon become tiresome. I'm rather keen on the 'fake' idea, which adds a touch of sophistication to the concept. A fake rose tree, covered in dark green moss and foliage and dotted with roses, could be fun. So might fake box trees, made of small-leaved foliage, or a moss-covered tree with dark hydrangea blooms. If you would like to make trees of your own, large

or small, there are full instructions on page 68.

Finally, to a very individual bathroom. Like kitchens, bathrooms aren't normally considered to be the best place for dried flowers. But there are bathrooms and bathrooms, and this one is not the small, steamy type and so it is a perfectly practical place to have dried flowers. Several small arrangements were made to dot around the room. On the left, in front of the bird cage, is a tree with two flowering heads. The flowers include roses, botao buttons, glixia, titree and carthamus, with the pink spikes of *Paranomus sphathulatus*.

Hanging from the dresser are three flower pomanders, all variations on the same colour theme. Pomanders like these are easy to make. Just take a commercially produced sphere of dry foam (if you can't find one in the right size you can carve your own from a larger block) and, resting it on a table, cover it with a selection of flowers keeping them packed tightly to prevent any gaps showing through. To finish the bottom, take a length of ribbon and a long, firm wire – if necessary, join two wires together. Bend the wire into a U-shape, then stick the ends through the ribbon and into the pomander, pushing them right through until they emerge at the bottom. Bend them upwards and back into the foam. This will hold the ribbon firmly in position. Hang the pomander up and finish covering it with flowers. Fragrance can be added with a few drops of essential oil applied either directly to the foam or to the flowers. Add more oil to refresh the pomander as and when it's needed.

An old chamber-pot forms the container for the main arrangement. The bathroom seemed an appropriate place

*Linking house and garden, a pair
of dried-flower daisy trees in
perfect counterpoint each side of a
well-framed door*

*A chamber-pot and a jug and basin set make inspired containers for this
sophisticated bathroom. Sponges and loofah-type material are the
starting point for the main arrangement, while fragrance is supplied by
the perfumed pomanders and the lavender-filled basin.*

for a display of flowers with a watery theme, centred on sponges against a background of coral fans, shells (contributed from her collection by my daughter, Sophie) and assorted bits of loofah-type material. Echoing the prickly textures are globe thistles, banksia heads and caustus, while pink-dyed botao heads add bright patches of colour that hold the arrangement together. All of our sponges and materials came from a specialist supplier, but one could just as easily use the kind of natural sponges and loofahs commercially available in most chemists' and drug stores.

While we were working out what kind of accessories to use for this bathroom photograph, our stylist brought out an attractive basin and jug set, which were instantly seized upon and taken to the work-room. There a mossed garland was attached to the rim using florists' tape (see page 134) on the delicate porcelain, and small bunches of roses, carthamus, amaranthus and lavender were wired into place. The bowl was filled with lavender and the jug placed in it. Once again we had a successful and surprise arrangement inspired by an unusual container.

I've mentioned the importance of containers elsewhere in this book, but it is worth repeating. Whatever it is – a porcelain jug sitting empty in a bedroom, an old wooden box used for storing toys, a junk-shop bargain you never quite knew what to do with – the right container will be the inspiration for something brilliantly original. When you're stuck for ideas for a special arrangement, don't just reach for a vase or a basket. Search the house and garden, climb up to the attic, excavate the junk cupboard for that one elusive and inspirational item that's just waiting there to be discovered.

Making the Arrangement

A DAISY TREE

In the spring and summer months two real daisy trees flank this doorway. For autumn and winter, when the plants are not at their best, we made this pair of trees to take their place. By varying the material used for flowers and foliage it's possible to achieve a wide variety of styles – anything from an almost real bay tree or standard rose bush to abstract designs in unnatural colours. The choice of trunk is almost as important as the foliage. A gnarled old apple branch creates one effect, a straight, slim beech branch another. Even when you are making small trees with trunks perhaps only a few inches tall, look for a piece of branch with a good shape or interesting bark texture. If you cut a fresh branch for your tree allow it to dry out for two weeks before you use it. Otherwise it may shrink and come loose from the plaster base.

At Armscote I like to use terracotta pots for our decorative trees. Not only do they look good, but they give weight and solidity to the finished tree. After blocking any drainage holes with a piece of card, the pots are filled with a mixture of thistle plaster (or strong wall plaster) and ozone-friendly polystyrene packaging bubbles, a combination discovered only after long experimentation. When it sets, plaster generates heat that can crack the pot. Once set, it shrinks. The polystyrene bubbles solve both problems, expanding and contracting with the plaster and gripping firmly to the walls of the pot to create a stable base. To finish the pot I usually fill the top with a layer of moss held in place with a few spots of glue. For something a little different you could use potpourri or, for a really splendid feature, make a dried-flower garland and attach it round the rim of the pot.

Once you've gone to the trouble of making a dried-flower tree it's a simple matter to refresh it if it begins to fade or to adapt it to suit a new location. By replacing the flowers with new material you can create a new tree to suit any setting.

MATERIALS REQUIRED
- *A large pot*
- *Thistle plaster*
- *Expanded polystyrene packaging bubbles*
- *Branch*
- *Mixing bowl and water*
- *Dry foam blocks*
- *Narrow tape*
- *Glue*
- *Scissors and a knife*
- *Stub wires*
- *Lupidium, ambrosinia or similar feathery green dried foliage, helipterums or other daisy-like material and sphagnum moss*

1 Mix the thistle plaster to a smooth, creamy consistency with water. Add the expanded polystyrene packaging bubbles – a handful for a small pot, more for a larger one. Pour the plaster mixture into the container and place the branch in the centre. Prop in position until set and trim to the size required.

2 Attach blocks of dry foam firmly to the branches using narrow tape and, if necessary, glue. When placing the blocks, bear in mind the finished shape you want to achieve.

3 Add the base material. We used lupidium, which has stiff stems that are easily inserted into the foam. For a more dense, bunched effect or when using softer material, wire a number of stems together (see page 118) and stick the wires into the foam.

4 Bunches of helipterum were wired in clusters of varying shapes and sizes and inserted randomly amongst the foliage to create the daisy-tree effect. To finish off place a layer of moss around the base of the tree so that the plaster mixture is not visible.

CHAPTER THREE

OUTDOOR PERSPECTIVE

According to the rules, dried flowers should not be used outdoors — but they make such a wonderful contrast to the natural materials found there, weathered stone, mellow brick and wood, that it would be a shame not to break the rules occasionally. I particularly like to use them for special celebrations, when their sheer impracticality adds to the sense of occasion.

Simple bunches and buckets of flowers in a rustic lean-to. Strictly speaking dried flowers should not be used outdoors — but having seen how good they look here, who could fail to be tempted?

EXTERIORS

Dried flowers outdoors? Dried flowers for decorating front doors, porches – a gazebo? Were we crazy?

There were several sceptical glances when I suggested that we include a chapter on exteriors in this book. 'But what if it rains?' everyone asked. I will be the first to admit that dried flowers are not the most practical way of decorating an exterior feature. Neither are fresh flowers. If practicality is everything, we should head straight for plastic fakes. But dried flowers can look wonderful outdoors for special occasions. And if one takes reasonable care and doesn't expect them to be a permanent fixture, then why not use them?

As the picture on the previous page shows, you don't have to design elaborate formal arrangements to achieve a very pleasing effect. We took this photograph in the delightfully ramshackle lean-to of a manor house only a few miles from Armscote. It's a working farm producing wonderful organic lamb, and its owner has no intention of turning it into a design showpiece. But when we used it to display a selection of dried and fresh flowers it was utterly transformed. There are no clever or wildly original arrangements here, just a few dried bunches hanging casually from a post, some old buckets containing a variety of dried vegetables and garden flowers and some fresh artichokes, peonies, eryngium, honesty and leek heads all hanging up to dry. But they're appropriate to the functional appearance of the lean-to and, without making it look too fussy or unnatural, quietly make it a more attractive feature of the house.

There's no point in being unrealistic about using dried flowers outside. They obviously survive best in dry, airy conditions and out of direct sunlight, which destroys their natural colour. Bunches and bucket arrangements left under the shelter of this lean-to for the summer would probably end up battered, bleached and, if it was a poor year, damp and perhaps rotten. But if one chooses tough and what I rather unflatteringly call 'expendable' materials, then this doesn't really matter. The plants I have in mind are those that grow abundantly in most gardens – achillea, helichrysums, sea lavender, statice, eryngium, nigella, catmint, marjoram – all flowers that are useful fillers for arrangements but are not highly-prized; flowers that might perhaps be left on the plant if you already had enough of them dried and in store. Save roses, delphiniums and the more delicate and rare material for indoor use, but cut and dry these less special plants for use outdoors. Wildflowers such as buttercups and cow parsley (also known rather more elegantly as Queen Anne's lace) can be found in hedgerows and untended land, and used in sheltered exterior spots throughout the summer. They can then be thrown away later in the year or, if they've survived the experience, added to interior arrangements.

This all rather takes it for granted that you will be drying your own flowers. It's not necessary to do so, of course. There are excellent suppliers of dried flowers to be found in most areas these days (see page 135). But if you have a garden, do try it. It's the kind of task, like embroidering cushion covers or making your own preserves, that isn't strictly necessary but does give a great sense of personal satisfaction.

If you don't have a garden then you can buy bunches of roses, cornflowers, peonies and larkspur in summer, when they are plentiful, and dry them at home. Or you could try asking friends and neighbours if you could cut an armful of alchemilla or nigella, or a few hydrangea heads from their garden. You might even consider an informal business arrangement with a keen local gardener, so that he grows a few flowers each year specially for you. The results will be worth it, I promise. Your own carefully dried and tended flowers will be in much better condition and have a fresher look than bought material. And, something I value when I use my own home-grown flowers, the arrangements you make from them will hold memories for you – of a visit to a friend's garden, a surprise bouquet, an afternoon spent gathering moss in the forest.

All fresh material, whatever its source, should be properly dried before it's used for arrangements anywhere, indoors or out. There are several different drying methods (see page 130 for further details) but the simplest and most common method used is air drying. This is the process we employ most widely at Armscote and is the easiest for using at home. Divide freshly-cut material into bunches of four or five stems (leave large flowers or seed heads – artichokes, for example – single) and secure with twine. Hang them upside down somewhere warm, dark and dry with plenty of circulating air (see page 130). When I first started the business at Armscote we dried tons of home-grown flowers in this way in one of the barns. Today we require such quantities that we are forced to buy them in from local and foreign sources, but we still dry some of the more delicate material on the premises. When both flowers and stalks have dried out, which can take anything from a week to over a month, the material is ready to be used. By adding a little heat to the circulating air this process can be speeded up, and I find the quality and colour of the flowers is improved.

Examples of the vast variety of materials that can be dried and the uses to which they can be put are illustrated in the more detailed picture of the lean-to overleaf. The contents of the bicycle basket displays some of the riches

Sunlight, wind and rain are all natural enemies of dried flowers, and one can't expect dried materials used out of doors to last for long. But if you choose the toughest and most abundant varieties from your garden – achillea, eryngium and poppies, for example – and use them in a sheltered spot, it's possible to make an effective display that has a chance of withstanding the elements. Here the easiest of all arrangements, hanging bunches, help to transform a functional lean-to into an attractive feature of the house.

freely available in a well-planned garden. At the front is a bunch of green honesty. Honesty is so easy to grow and dry that its papery brown seed heads have become a terrible cliché in the flower-arranging world. This seems a pity because it can be very attractive, particularly at this stage when it has such a good colour. Dried carefully, in the dark, it should retain its greenness.

Next to it in the basket are the extraordinary conical seed heads of *Allium siculum,* a hardy bulb growing up to four feet high. In early summer it produces attractive white bell-shaped flowers which have tinges of green and purple. Once the blooms are over the seed heads can be cut for drying and make a strikingly structural contribution to arrangements. By the side of these are the bulbous seed heads of the beautiful orange and yellow Peruvian lily, alstroemeria, which makes a bold splash of colour in the garden throughout the summer. They are backed by fresh-cut green poppy heads which turn to silvery blue when dry.

The little basket on the wall is full of fresh flowers waiting to be prepared for drying. The gorgeous bright yellow-green of alchemilla, beloved of all flower arrangers, is an excellent foil to the dark, spiny stems of acanthus, which look very dramatic once dried. Tucked in with them are bunches of golden-yellow buttercups, which keep their colour well after drying, and shaggy-textured leek heads, perfect for large-scale arrangements.

Rich pickings from the garden. A bicycle basket is packed with freshly-picked seedheads while alchemilla, buttercups, peonies and leek heads wait to be dried. On the left is the Armscote Manor alternative windowbox, with flowers arranged by my husband Fred and daughter Sophie.

The bucket, at ground level, contains a prickly selection of maize and artichokes, both of which can be preserved by air drying. They'll take longer than most other materials to dry out, but the results are worth waiting for. In with them are silver-blue globe thistles and the large daisy-style flower heads of the carline thistle.

Above this, in an extremely battered wooden trough exhumed from one of the old greenhouses at Armscote, is a whimsical arrangement that looks quite at home in this rustic setting. I've mentioned the important part containers play in inspiring ideas previously, and this old box is yet another example of an unlikely container giving life to an unconventional but successful arrangement.

The idea was originally sparked off by someone who was looking for unusual windowboxes to photograph for a book. We couldn't help with a real windowbox, but the idea stayed with us and we made this one instead. Because we wanted to make something a little more interesting than a traditional windowbox, we filled the trough with terracotta pots of all shapes and sizes, old ones, new ones, broken ones – everything we could find around the garden. These were packed with moss and then Fred and Sophie spent a pleasant hour or two finishing them off with the most unlikely and colourful selection of odds and ends they could lay their hands on. One could, of course, have filled them with a more realistic selection of flowers and leaves, so that the box looked as if it was full of growing plants. I think our version is great fun, a family arrangement, packed with an eclectic combination of smoke bush, lavender, achillea, roses, globe amaranth, carthamus, buttercups, poppies . . . the list goes on. For anyone who has ever palled at the price of a large, eye-catching arrangement I offer this as an example of the kind of thing one can make almost for free.

One couldn't, alas, say the same of the dried flowers

used to dress the gazebo at Armscote for a spring party, shown opposite. It's lovely to have such an elegant feature in the garden and great fun to use it for a special occasion, particularly when we can make it look this good. Naturally we wouldn't have decorated it if the weather had been bad, but fate smiled on us; the day was fine and the garlands and pots survived not only the party but also the night, apparently quite unscathed by dew. I wouldn't recommend leaving them out for any longer than this without some form of protection, but I think dried material is considerably tougher and more tolerant than we imagine. If it does get wet, dry it immediately in warm, dark, airy conditions. As long as it hasn't been soaked through it should look relatively unscathed.

When it came to deciding on material for decorating an English country garden we couldn't think of anything better than roses and lavender which were incorporated freely into the arrangements. The basic designs were very simple, based on a background of dark green sparsa interspersed with lighter green caustus. This scheme was carried all the way through, with a few additions. To the large and relatively free arrangement at the back of the gazebo we added acanthus branches with some of their white flowers still attached. These almost imperceptible touches help to lighten the arrangement. It is important when you are working on an arrangement of this scale, particularly one that is not going to be seen from close quarters, to use your dried flowers as if they were paint, adding broad strokes and large splashes of colour, rather than diluting the effect with too much detail.

We used more of the acanthus, with its spiky, distinctive shape, in the stone pots in front of the gazebo. To these were added strong green eucalyptus leaves, which echoed the shape and colour of the bluebells in the flower-beds. The finished effect was quite magical, well worth the effort and admired by everyone who saw it. Hard work, maybe, but it turned a pleasant evening into something memorable.

It's almost a crime to intrude on the scene with thoughts about the practicality of using dried flowers like this, but that's inevitably the kind of question that springs to most people's minds. The good news is that something like this need not be wasteful or extravagant if one plans it so that the materials and arrangements can be re-used. All the flowers could have been taken down and stored until the next garden party, for example – try doing that with fresh flowers! Or if the next special occasion is too far off to merit storing them, they could be used indoors. Those beautiful stone pots could be taken straight in to stand each side of a hearth, or on a landing. The garlands, too, would make a spectacularly romantic feature in a bedroom or, with the roses quickly removed and holly and silver balls wired in place, a wonderful Christmas decoration for the hall or living-room. And the material from the back of the gazebo could be incorporated into a wide variety of arrangements – anything from a large and beautiful basket to a standard rose tree or two. There need, in fact, be no waste at all.

The gazebo at Armscote Manor decorated for a spring party. Treat arrangements like these as purely temporary exterior features and bring them into the house as soon as you can.

OUT OF DOORS

There are some occasions, of course, when extravagance is in order, and a wedding is one of them. It's difficult to think of a better way of welcoming the wedding party to the church than by decorating the entrance with flowers, and that's exactly what we did (see left) at St James the Great's, a tiny twelfth-century church in Idlicote, just up the road from Armscote. (To see how we coped with the interior turn to page 88.)

The garland arranged around the porch matches the one we used inside. It's a broad and very richly textured arrangement, full of brilliant red roses, hydrangeas, lilac achillea, statice, larkspur and celosia. The weather was good enough for us to pin it outside the porch on the day, but had it been raining or damp we would simply have moved it further inside and draped it around the door. Hung as it was, it made an excellent frame for the happy couple when they emerged after the service and posed for photographs.

In an unashamedly romantic gesture we hung a huge bow entirely covered in flowers on the church door. The top half was moulded from chicken wire and moss to make a flat pad, which was then studded with flowers. The hanging ties, covered in red-brown titree, were made from two lengths of mossed garland, with a flower-covered sphere

What better way to welcome guests to a wedding than with glorious flowers framing the church porch? A garland like this can be made well in advance and put up in just a few minutes. It creates an attractive backdrop for photographs after the service, and when the wedding is over it can be used to decorate the couple's home – a reminder of that very special day.

of dry foam at the end of each. A little over the top, perhaps, but all the more fun for that.

Of all the external features of a house, I think the front door is the most obvious and easy to decorate. So why not go ahead and do something with it? It's frivolous and unnecessary, true, but then so are many of the most satisfying things in life. A wreath or a garland on the front door is attractive and fun, a good way of greeting people as they arrive for a party or a special celebration. And when the party's over you can take down your exterior dried-flower arrangements and hang them up indoors.

The picture on page 80 shows the front door at Armscote Manor in summer splendour. In the four hundred years or thereabouts it has been here, I doubt whether it has ever looked quite so decorative. The garlands that hang each side of the door are full of mimosa and wonderfully exotic-looking lotus pods. At the bottom of each is a small oat sheaf, which echoes the larger sheaf pinned to the door itself. When the flowers are taken down they can be hung inside the hall, with the sheaf perhaps pinned to the back of the door.

Our front door is studded with ancient nails on which to hang such a sheaf or wreath, but if yours is not, and you don't want to damage it by hammering a pin into it then you can secure an arrangement by using fishing line and a drawing pin. Open the door wide and insert the tack or pin into the top edge, where a hole won't show. Press it down firmly, then try the door to ensure that it will still shut. (Most doors have sufficient gap at the top to allow this.) Cut a length of fishing line, loop it round the tack and bring it down the exterior of the door. Take the arrangement, thread the fishing-line through the wires at the back of it and secure it in the position required. The fishing line

ABOVE *The front door at Armscote Manor, decorated with garlands of mimosa, lotus seed heads and an oat sheaf. Frivolous, impractical, but a great way of welcoming guests to a party or marking a special occasion.* RIGHT *The freshest, most crisp arrangement in this book. Green Granny Smith apples set the tone for this spectacular double wreath decorated in sharp greens and white. We used the unusual double shape because we wanted an alternative to the traditional plain round wreath.*

will be almost invisible and the arrangement should hang safely, and without damaging the door.

Fishing line was not strong enough to support the last of our exterior arrangements photographed on page 81. It took a two-inch (5cm) nail to secure this apple-covered wreath, which contains at least six pounds of Granny Smith apples, to the door. It was the sharp colour of the apples that inspired the arrangement; the double-wreath shape developed because we were determined not to make an ordinary, single round one. Sometimes a stubborn refusal to do what's expected leads to very attractive results, as shown here. The top wreath is a crisp combination of colours that we would not normally think subtle enough to combine. White larkspur and helichrysums stand out boldly against the strong, clear greens of alchemilla, dyed glixia, white gypsophila and both standard and miniature varieties of honesty. The effect is brilliantly fresh and clean, positively mouthwatering.

The apples are simply pierced with wires and secured to a moss-covered wreath frame. They may last several weeks before drying out or beginning to rot. When this happens they can be removed and replaced, if desired, with a more durable material. Bunches of green-dyed or white botao buttons, or clumps of white helichrysums would also look striking against the dark green of the sphagnum moss.

Making the Arrangement
A ROPE GARLAND

Garlands are a wonderful way of decorating large areas of space and awkward places. You can wind them around banisters and handrails for a speedy transformation of the plainest staircase, spiral them around an old gazebo as we did, or drape them around doorways and picture frames. Wherever you use them their effect is always dramatic and extravagant.

The basic material needed to make a rope garland is, predictably enough, a rope. Use nylon rope as it is lighter and cheaper than other types. The diameter will influence the width of the finished garland, but for most purposes half an inch is suitable. The best way of finding the right length for your garland or swag is not to measure with a ruler or tape, but to drape the naked rope across the wall, down the staircase, round the gazebo, or wherever, and then cut it to size. For covering the rope you will need plenty of sphagnum moss. This can be bought from florists (see page 135) or you can gather it yourself. We collect some of the moss used at Armscote from a secret location in woods not far away, and its colour and texture are far better than the bought variety. It's best to use the freshly-gathered moss while it's still damp, as it is easier to handle, but let it dry out before adding the dried material.

In this demonstration you'll see how to make the garland we used for decorating the gazebo, but you can vary the contents as much as you like.

MATERIALS REQUIRED
- *Length of half-inch (1.2cm) nylon rope*
- *Reel wire and stub wires*
- *Scissors*
- *Sphagnum moss, fern, roses, caustus and lavender*

1 Bend a stub wire into a U-shape and attach it to the end of the rope with reel wire (see page 134) to make a loop from which the garland can be hung. Taking a handful of moss, bind it firmly around the rope with the reel wire. Add further clumps of moss, binding it in as you go with one continuous spiral of wire. Build up a thick layer that covers the rope completely. Add another hanging loop at the far end of the rope.

2 Take your basic material, in this case dried fern, and gather a few stems together to form a fan shape. Place this bunch at the end of the rope, covering the hanging loop, and bind it tightly with reel wire. Take the next bunch of fern, place it so that it slightly overlaps the first bunch and conceals the wires, and bind this in position also. Continue until the top of the whole rope is covered – don't bother with the underside, which will not be seen.

3 Make up small bunches of roses, caustus and lavender with stub wires. Allow a bunch of three roses for roughly every six inches of garland. Insert the roses at regular intervals along the garland, pushing the wires through the moss layer, out the other side and then threading the ends back into the moss.

4 Add the caustus and the lavender in the same way. Inspect the garland for visible wires and adjust the foliage and flowers to cover them. Hang the garland and check that the materials are evenly distributed. Adjust if necessary.

Chapter Four

SPECIAL OCCASIONS

A winter wedding, a traditional Christmas celebration, a harvest or thanksgiving supper are just a few of the occasions when one is justified in going over the top with dried flowers. Used generously, they add a touch of magic and fantasy to any scene. And they're not just a spectacularly beautiful way of decorating a house, church or barn; they are also eminently practical arrangements on the kind of truly lavish scale that will totally transform a setting.

Country bunches and red rope make a simple but very effective display across the altar rail. Beneath the window a wide garland creates a tapestry of contrasting colours, while to the side of the altar a huge, free arrangement fills an awkward area of white space.

A WINTER WEDDING

A crisp winter's day, blue sky and sunshine. A twelfth-century church hidden down a quiet country lane. Brides-maids in red velvet dresses. And the interior of the church glowing with dried garlands and bunches of red roses massed with rich coppers, blues, green, pinks . . . These are the ingredients for a perfect winter wedding.

It's difficult to imagine a more charming location for a small wedding than the church of St James the Great at Idlicote, just a few miles down the road from Armscote. Built in the twelfth and late thirteenth centuries, it has a wealth of historical detail, including a large, high-sided pew where the local squire and his family would have sat out of sight of the lowlier members of the congregation. Another major feature, which we chose to highlight with our decorations, is the triple-decker pulpit. The sermon is read from the canopied top deck and the service taken from the lectern below. The lowest lectern, at the front of the pews, would originally have been occupied by the clerk who led the congregation. This area of the Cotswolds abounds with delightful churches, but few can rival the unspoilt charm of this one.

It's always saddened me that when it comes to special occasions, such as weddings, many people approach dried flowers as a last resort, a disappointing alternative to fresh flowers. I prefer to think of them as different, not second best. It's a bit like comparing the use of watercolours and oils in a painting. They're used in different ways for different effects. The same is true of dried flowers. Used creatively, dried flowers can offer tremendous scope for large-scale decorations. This is largely due to the fact that they're so practical to work with. All the arrangements you see in our pictures were made well in advance of the wedding day; we didn't have to worry about wilting and water-ing and all the other problems involved in working with fresh materials. And because we had the advantage of time, we could afford to be more lavish and imaginative than might otherwise have been the case.

Just a few words here about decorating churches. It's always advisable, no matter how low-key your flowers, to check with the clergyman concerned that it is all right for you to use them. There may be guidelines on the type of fixings you are allowed to use; some churches have been damaged by the indiscriminate hammering-in of nails and pins. If the church is a particularly busy one, there may also be a limit to the amount of time you have to put up and later remove the decorations between services. All these things should be taken into account before one starts plan-ning the flowers.

Once these details have been sorted out, one can move on to specific decisions, such as what colours to use. The fact that we were working with dried flowers in-fluenced our choice. We could have chosen to follow the traditional look and used pink roses, gypsophila, sea lavender, peonies, and larkspur to make pale, pretty arrangements. Instead we decided to go for something quite different; a spectrum of rich, glowing colours to provide warmth and brightness on a cold day. This is where dried flowers really come into their own. Their strong colours and textures can be used to create a kind of drama that is difficult to achieve with fresh materials. In these circumstances dried flowers aren't a substitute for the real thing – they're the first and best choice.

Looking for key themes on which to base the arrangements, we took into consideration the occasion and the style of the church and chose romantic red roses and bows, country bunches and warm-textured velvet. I find this technique of starting with a few basic elements very useful. Once the themes of a design have been established, the details then seem to fall quickly into place. I also find it useful to walk around the work-room and shop gathering a colour swatch of flowers and trying different combinations together until I have a small posy containing all the shades and forms that will be used. This is kept as a reference while we plan and make-up the arrangements. You can do this too, incorporating swatches of fabric and paint colours with small samples of dried flowers to work out a variety of combinations. A good dried flower shop should be happy to supply you with samples from which to choose.

Once we had decided upon our themes, colours and materials, we began designing the actual arrangements. For the altar rail, shown in the picture on pages 84-5, we used simple country bunches of single and spray red roses, nigella, sea lavender, dark red helichrysums, rust-coloured lupidium, green eucalyptus and large creamy-brown hoya leaves. These were trimmed with sumptuous wired bows of red velvet and hung along the altar rail at intervals. We added a long rope of ruched velvet to link them together, much of which was sewn by my husband, whose skill with the needle came as a great surprise! Each of the bunches was made by a member of the Armscote team, and although they all used the same materials they assembled them in slightly different ways. This was done deliberately. It's impossible to make two arrangements look exactly alike, so I prefer to use the differences positively and allow each its own character.

Something much larger was needed to fill the area of white space to the left of the altar and so we created an informal arrangement based around bunches of roses. We used both sprays of rambling roses and the larger individual blooms to give a variety of density and form. Glycerined green and copper beech branches were used

for height and volume, while the silver leaves of weeping pear can be seen at the bottom of the arrangement. Small bunches of oats and quaking grass gave a lift to the top, while the silver-white strands of seacrest helped break up the heavier foliage and provided a link with the white walls. The result is a big splash of rich, muted colour that boldly fills a difficult space.

I've found that it's best to build this kind of arrangement *in situ* so that one can judge exactly how large it needs to be for the best effect – which is usually much larger than originally anticipated. Remember that very few people are going to get close to it, so be brave and aim for a dramatic overall impression, like we did with the gazebo, rather than fine detail.

Across the carved screen and panelling behind the altar runs a wide garland packed with roses, both red and pink, hydrangeas in shades of purple, pale blue and light green, rust-coloured celosia, nigella, purple and mauve

A rich garland wound across the screen of the church helps to break-up the height of the arch and forms a glowing frame for the couple at the altar. The red velvet bows and the rope, used here and throughout the church, are touches of inspired colour that link all the arrangements together and contribute to the warm atmosphere in the church.

statice, pink African daisies, reddish-brown lupidium and lilac achillea, interspersed with glycerined poplar leaves dyed a strong blue-green. Here and there patches of sky-blue and pale pink reindeer moss fill up gaps between the flowers and add bright spots of unexpected colour that lift the darker hues of the garland. The result is a close-woven tapestry of colour and texture, full of contrasts and details.

A length of the same garland, interwoven with more of the red velvet rope, makes a spectacular feature of the carved wooden screen that spans the main arch. It can be appreciated in closer detail in the picture overleaf. Manoeuvring it into position and wrapping it at regular intervals across the screen was a major undertaking, but the garland stood up well to the stresses and strains. Remember another of the advantages of dried flowers is that they are more robust than they look. Whatever the effort, it was well worth it. The garland-covered screen provided a visual link between the two areas of the church and made a beautiful frame above the bride and groom at the altar.

The base of this broad garland is made of large-gauge chicken wire cut into a strip approximately 14 inches (35cm) wide. A word of warning is needed here as moulding chicken wire into shape can be a difficult process, so I would suggest wearing gardening gloves while you're handling it; especially as the cut ends can be very sharp. Tightly-packed dry sphagnum moss is then placed in the centre of the chicken wire and the edges folded inwards and secured, if necessary, with wire. This 'moss sausage' is flattened to make a firm, flat base about six inches (15cm) wide into which the flowers are wired. The final result is a reasonably flexible but secure garland, which will stand up to being twisted and pulled about without shedding its flowers.

Echoing this large garland is a narrower one that runs along the ledge in front of the choir stall. This was constructed on a mossed rope (see page 82 for details of how to make this kind of garland). It contains red roses, celosia, dark red helichrysums, blue-violet larkspur, nigella, pale pink African daisies and fronds of dried fern. Pale silver-blue poppy heads have been added for extra texture and interest. I like this idea of using two slightly different garlands in the same setting. Watching the people who came into the church while we were decorating it, I noticed how many of them examined the wide garland on the screen, compared it with the rope garland and then returned to the wide garland, to check its contents again. They would repeat this several times and each time they commented upon the differences their inspections had revealed.

When it comes to measuring up for garlands, I recommend using a rope, as I explained on page 82, since it's far easier to twine a rope around a screen or along a ledge and to measure off the length than it is to gauge it with a tape measure or ruler. I also find it helpful to take a few photographs at this stage, so that I can refer back to them if problems arise later. This is a particularly good idea if you can't keep returning to the place you're decorating. It's easy to forget the exact position of a pillar or a window. With a photograph for reference you can usually work out where you've gone wrong.

We used the rope technique for measuring up the swags that hang around the pulpit (see opposite) and

When there's a feature as splendid as this triple-decker pulpit, one simply has to make use of it. We did so with swags and narrow garlands that echo, but don't copy, the wide one overhead. For the panels of the old-fashioned box pews, alternating country bunches and bows add rustic simplicity and a touch of witty sophistication.

once the basic shape of each swag was established using roughly shaped pads made out of chicken wire, we wired in a selection of flowers. Clumps of dyed reindeer moss, secured with a wire bent into a simple U-shape were also added to the pad.

To break up the dull brown varnish of the box pews we hung alternating rows of bunches and bows along the panels. Like the swags, the basic shape of each bow was provided by a pad made out of chicken wire and moss and scrunched into shape. It's possible to achieve surprisingly detailed shapes using this technique. The bows were finished with long tails of red velvet.

Finally, the edge of the lower lectern was draped with another length of the rope garland, and further bunches were strategically placed to break up areas of white wall. When you're decorating a large and complicated space such as a church, it's always a good idea to take along more material than you think you will need – an extra length of garland, a few bunches, and a box of loose flowers may prove invaluable for filling an awkward gap. Despite advance planning there are always empty spaces and spots which need to be filled or concealed.

Our bridal bouquet, shown opposite, matches the strong statement made by the rest of our arrangements. It was packed with red roses, glycerined ivy, eucalyptus and beech leaves and large *Protea sulphurea*, with skeletal magnolia leaves. Bleached strelitzia and twisted cane gave it lightness and movement. It is boldly romantic and not for the faint-hearted. We designed it on a grand scale to sweep down to the feet of a tall bride, but a more restrained version would look just as good and one could use the same materials for making the bridesmaids' posies.

When making a bouquet like this, begin by establishing the length and general shape with foliage, gradually building up the layers and changing the angle of the flowers as you go. You may need to use several lengths of thick florists' wire joined together to achieve the right drop. Cover the wires with gutta percha (see page 134) to give them a neater finish. Gather all the wires and stalks at the back of the bouquet to make a handle and secure them into shape. Then cover the handle with gutta percha, line it with cotton wool or tissue paper and finally cover with ribbon. For fun and to echo the exposed stalks of the country bunches hanging on the pews, we added a false spray of stalks and a huge red bow to our bouquet. The end result was both dramatic and delightfully informal, a bouquet for making an unforgettable entrance to the church. And unlike one made from fresh flowers, it can be kept as a reminder of that perfect winter wedding.

To match the bouquet we made a simple, very free headdress from a wreath of lime twigs trimmed with celosia, stirlingia, fir cones, *Protea sulphurea*, pink and red miniature roses and touches of seacrest. This was decorated with another large velvet bow to be worn at the back or the side of the head. Dyed lichen moss was wired around the interior to allow a comfortable fit.

It's important when making a headdress like this to know how the bride intends to wear her hair on the wedding day and whether she will want to attach a veil. If this is the case, the veil can be sewn into the back of the circlet.

For a final touch to a perfect wedding, you might also like to consider decorating the church porch with a garland of flowers (see page 79).

This unashamedly romantic bouquet provides one of the finishing touches for the winter wedding. Though it takes its main colour inspiration from the red roses used elsewhere in the church, it is full of subtle contrasts.

Making the Arrangement

A BRIDE'S HEADDRESS

A coronet of flowers, whether fresh or dried, makes a classic and fashionable headdress for a bride and her bridesmaids. Be brave when making a circlet like this. Weddings are theatrical occasions and the headdress needs to be full and dramatic. It is the bride's crowning glory, not a last-minute afterthought. Experiment with different ways of wearing it until you find the angle that looks best, and remember to make the back just as beautiful as the front.

The circlet I'm demonstrating here incorporates the colours and materials we selected for the winter wedding, but you can use whatever you like when you make your own. When choosing materials, look for a variety of different textures and some contrasting colours. If you want to include the dense, velvety textures of moss and celosia, use something light and airy such as seacrest or gypsophila to balance them. If you choose pretty pinks as the basic colour, add sharp-green caustus or the silver-turquoise of baby eucalyptus.

Lime is particularly suitable for making the basic wreath, but you can use other types of pliable materials. A simple wire ring, completely covered with flowers and lichen, would be a perfectly good substitute.

MATERIALS REQUIRED
- *Lime twigs*
- *Stub and reel wire*
- *Scissors*
- *Gutta percha*
- *A velvet bow*
- *Roses, celosia, Decorum fir cones, Protea sulphurea, seacrest, fern and dyed reindeer moss*

1 Take a bunch of lime twigs and bend one to make a circle with a diameter of approximately 10-12 inches (25-30cm). Wire it into shape. Weave in further twigs, tucking them into position if possible, and wiring them only where necessary as it is important to keep the wiring to a minimum. Build up the circlet and trim any loose ends.

2 Add large-scale flowers, for example, seacrest, to the circlet. Divide materials such as celosia into florets. Wire-up small bunches of all the materials and cover the wires with gutta percha to conceal the joins. Combine individual small bunches to make sprays which are wired to the circlet at intervals.

3 Position the sprays at different angles so there is no obvious direction. Use materials at random so that the look is not too uniform. Add cones, Protea sulphurea and reindeer moss to cover the stalks and wires.

4 Stick or wire some more of the moss over any sharp interior twigs. Wire the bow into position at the back or side of the wreath.

AN EASTER CELEBRATION

Yellow is the colour of springtime – of daffodils, prim-roses, chicks on Easter eggs, and warm sunshine after the long, dark, winter days – and so it's the obvious choice for Easter flowers. Very few of us go to such lengths to dec-orate our homes for the Easter festival as we do for Christ-mas, but it's still nice to mark the occasion. And the nicest way is with an arrangement or two for the breakfast or tea table on Easter Sunday.

Easter Sunday breakfast tends to be an informal affair, especially if you have children, and so I like the arrangements to reflect this relaxed atmosphere. It is also a great opportunity to make use of all those charming, mis-matched, amusing items of china that most of us have around our homes.

For our arrangements we collected together various pieces of country ware; a teapot, jugs and a biscuit barrel, all in the shape of cottages, an old jam pot, a pixie jug and a pitcher shaped like a cockerel. Interesting old mugs and cups and the kind of whimsical containers that are difficult to know what to do with the rest of the year all come in use-ful at Eastertime. So do eggcups. A very pretty display can be made using a variety of eggcups filled with dry foam and studded with flowers. Children love making this sort of simple arrangement. For something a little more special for an Easter guest, take a double eggcup and fill one side of it with flowers. In the other place a decorated boiled egg.

The photograph on the right demonstrates the easy and yet very attractive results one can achieve with the minimum of sophistication. On the left yellow helichry-sums, green glixia, lavender, phalaris, yellow-dyed gyp-sophila and creamy-white pearl achillea were combined to create this sunny effect. In front of it, another small jug

was filled with yellow roses, purple larkspur, cluster-flowered *Helipterum sanfordii*, small-headed achillea, im-mortellum and oats. A third jug contains a mixture of this material combined with some strong green eucalyptus leaves to give the arrangement new colour and shape.

Small arrangements like these are an excellent way for a beginner to learn basic dried-flower arranging skills and develop confidence. For your first attempt at knitting you wouldn't start with a complicated Fairisle sweater, yet some people attempt the dried-flower equivalent. Fired with enthusiasm after seeing a splendid basket or bouquet, they set out to produce their own version. Disillusionment soon creeps in as they discover how long it takes to finish and how difficult it can be to balance colours, shapes and textures to obtain what originally seemed a very simple effect. It's far better to start on a less ambitious project such as these small arrangements, which enable you to ex-periment with colour and shape as you go along. And even more important than this, small arrangements that use a wide variety of materials allow you to become familiar with the way in which different flowers work in com-bination with one another. You can try out new and daring ideas safe in the knowledge that if they don't work you won't have wasted huge amounts of flowers and that it won't take long to put it right.

The photograph on pages 98-99 demonstrates a few more of the possible variations on the Easter theme. Beneath the cockerel, now boasting a magnificent tail of dried flowers, is a jam pot filled with a mushroom-shaped mound of glixia arranged in irregular-shaped patches – a simple concept but one which demands dexterity and good colour sense. The two cottage arrangements have had flax, botao, carthamus and alchemilla added to ring the

Charming country-style jugs make ideal containers for bright, informal Easter arrangements like these. Make a feature of them by grouping a number together on a dresser or the breakfast table. Small-scale arrangements are the best way of gaining flower-arranging experience, allowing the beginner plenty of scope to experiment with colour and shape whilst guaranteeing fast results.

Variations on the Easter theme. Country cottages, plump yellow chicks and formal table arrangements are all linked by a common colour scheme and a few key materials.

changes. On the right is a more formal arrangement in a vase, showing how the same principles and materials can be used on a larger scale.

In the centre of the picture you'll see a large, low arrangement incorporating colourful polyanthus. This is our year-round table arrangement in its spring finery, ready to be used as a centrepiece on a dining-table or as an attractive, seasonal feature for elsewhere in the house.

The history of this arrangement, its constituents and the various ways in which it can be used are recounted in detail on page 114. Of course, you don't have to add polyanthus to it; any spring flowers or foliage will do. A combination of delicately scented narcissi, bright blue grape hyacinths and pink tulips would look wonderful. So would small sprigs of apple or cherry blossom and catkins. One advantage of using polyanthus is that, unlike cut flowers, they don't have to die to contribute their colour

and freshness to the arrangement. We took them from their pots, removed as much soil as possible from their roots and wrapped them gently in plastic film before adding them to the year-round arrangement. After several days they were taken out again and repotted, none the worse for their experience.

Finally we come to the most whimsical of all the Easter arrangements – our three plump yellow chicks in their nest. It's possible to make almost anything out of dried flowers, and what you make doesn't have to be serious or elegant. Teddy bears, rabbits, a model of the Empire State Building or a red London bus - there's no limit. Most arrangements of this kind are based on a frame made of chicken wire or a moss shape. In the case of our chicks, we started with two moss balls of different sizes, bound with reel wire. The two were combined to make the chick shape and then covered with individual florets of cluster-flowered helipterums which were stuck on with glue. A couple of small, pointed leaves were inserted to form the beak, and the eyes were made from the tiny seed heads of the field poppy, coloured black with a felt-tip pen.

Children are particularly enthusiastic about this literal use of dried flowers, which has a more immediate appeal for them than abstract arrangements. My daughter watched us taking hours over our nest of chicks and then produced a perfect specimen of her own in 15 minutes flat. And just to put us to further shame she also made it a little moss nest, in which it's sitting at this very moment in our kitchen waiting until it can assume pride of place next Easter!

A HARVEST FESTIVAL SUPPER

The barn shown on pages 106-107 is situated in the pretty village of Tredington just a mile or two down the road from Armscote. Usually it houses odd bits of furniture, bales of straw and the general bric-a-brac of farm life, but for special occasions it is cleared and used for parties. As soon as we saw its old beams and thatch we knew we'd found the perfect location for a harvest festival supper. Fortunately the barn's owners thought so too and very kindly allowed us to use it.

Dried flowers are a particularly appropriate medium for decorating a harvest festival. Like the fruit, vegetables and cereals on display, they're a tribute to nature's diversity and abundance. When it came to selecting flowers for the arrangements we bore this 'natural' theme in mind and deliberately tried to steer away from dyed, bleached or other 'unnatural' materials. We also tried to use the kind of autumn-tinted flowers one might expect to find in local cottage gardens and hedgerows, and aimed to make them into simple, unpretentious displays in keeping with the setting.

In order to achieve this we looked around for some simple, but rustic containers and, in keeping with the agricultural theme of the setting, agricultural tools. We were helped in our search for the latter by James Davis, an acquaintance who runs a marvellous antique shop in Shipston-on-Stour, our nearest town. He's a great enthusiast and collector of old agricultural implements and lent us some of his favourite items.

We started work in front of an old door, where the sunlight streaming through the gaps between the timbers created a wonderful pattern of light on our still-life grouping. Behind an old wheelbarrow filled with a variety of fresh vegetables we placed an apple tub packed with apples and decorated with bunches containing gnarled apple twigs, dark brown bracken, yellow broom and tufted phalaris. Next to it a basket taken from an old butcher's bicycle was filled with lavender. The front of the basket was trimmed with moss, bright yellow drumsticks of *Craspedia globosa* and dried delphiniums from the garden at Armscote.

Below it is one of the cheapest and simplest of all arrangements, a small wheatsheaf twisted, domed and tied with raffia. And proving my theory that one can use almost anything as a container and imaginative jumping-off point, the picture is completed by an old sack, something of a rarity in these days of plastic, topped with flowers – spray roses, poppy heads, oats, yellow daisies and *Limonium suworowii*, also known as pink poker. We stuffed the sack with newspapers to achieve the shape, then added a layer of crumpled chicken wire in which the flowers were inserted.

None of these arrangements required much expertise, time or money, yet all are effective. Perhaps the most distinctive harvest symbol of all is the wheatsheaf. Several sheaves, made in different sizes and of different cereals, grouped together would make a classic focus for a harvest thanksgiving service. Remember that the size of a sheaf is determined by its height. It's worth looking out for the taller varieties of wheat which will enable you to work on a larger scale.

There's another small wheatsheaf in the corner of the barn, but the attention here is focussed on two barrels decorated with wreaths of dried flowers, leaves and vegetables. It's the generous depth of these wreaths that make them look so good. Any narrower and they would have looked mean and insignificant. Any deeper and they would have been overwhelming.

Gauging proportions can be a difficult business, but I would always advise erring on the side of generosity. I think it's this that distinguishes the very best florists from the rest, both amateur and professional. The most dramatic and successful arrangements are those that very nearly go over the top. They are fuller, bigger, braver in colour and variety of materials than the rest. They make a strong, positive statement.

Bear this in mind when you are making an arrangement of your own. Nothing looks less interesting than a sparse scattering of flowers in boringly conventional complementary shades. Be brave and, when you think you've finished, try adding more flowers, some in a new and unexpected colour. Nine times out of ten the result is a great improvement on the original, and on the odd exception it's no great trouble to retrieve the basic arrangement and start all over again.

But back to our barrels. Both were prepared with a thick collar of dry sphagnum moss held in place by chicken wire which had been gathered and stapled, using a staple gun, to the inner rim. We then decorated one of the barrels in strong, autumn colours using golden helichry-

Dried flowers make an appropriate decoration for a harvest supper because, like so much of the fresh produce in the picture, many flowers and grasses are harvested for drying in the summer and early autumn. Of all the arrangements, the wheatsheaf is the quickest and easiest to make. Take a large bunch of wheat and tie it into a secure but slightly loose bundle. Now give the outer stems a firm twist so that they splay outwards in a spiral. Gradually push up the inner core of stems to create a softly rounded shape, then trim. Finish with raffia, a plaited straw garland or a paper bow.

sums, bright orange Chinese lanterns, yellow achillea and deep red celosia. The addition of brown bracken and oak leaves brought out the colour in the arrangement. Dark, sludgy, apparently unattractive colours often make the clearer, prettier colours around them sing. If you have a pretty but rather dull arrangement, try adding dark purple amaranthus, some deep copper beech leaves, rusty-purple dock or dark-dyed broom bloom and see what happens.

For the second barrel we used a quite different approach. Decorated in cool blues and greys with a sharp yellow, the result was sophisticated and muted: a contrast to the bright, sunny colours of the other arrangement. Dried artichokes, poppy heads and garlic all added to its strong sculptural qualities. The lemon helichrysums and verticordia formed a link with the other barrel, but the addition of lilac achillea, pale oats and dyed blue broom bloom changed the mood completely.

When planning a number of arrangements that will be grouped together, as here, it's tempting to stick to the same colours throughout so that everything is co-ordinated. The result can be pleasant but dull. Always include an occasional contrast, like this garlic-laden garland, to throw everything into perspective.

You don't have to be a colour expert to devise interesting combinations, but a little knowledge of the colour spectrum and the way it works can be useful. Generally speaking, colours that lie next to each other in the spectrum give a pleasing, low-key effect when used together. Thus, orange and yellow, yellow and green, green and blue, blue and violet, violet and red, and red and orange will blend harmoniously with each other. Colours a little further apart in the spectrum also combine well, but with a stronger contrast. Yellow and blue, green and violet, red and yellow, and orange and green, for example, are all striking and subtle combinations.

Most striking of all, and generally recommended only for the brave, are those colours which are furthest apart in the spectrum. Yellow and violet, red and green, and orange and blue combinations, will all result in startlingly dramatic effects that are best used with caution. These strong combinations are known as complementary colours; red is the complementary colour of green, and so on. To find out why they should be so called, try adding a red rose to a bunch of green eucalyptus leaves. The rose will make the eucalyptus appear even more green and will itself appear to be a truer red. The same is true of the yellow-violet and orange-blue combinations.

Complementary colours are particularly useful when you are trying to create special effects. A basket filled with orange dahlias, helichrysums and chinese lanterns, for example, will look brighter and more fiery if it is placed against a blue background, or if a few blue delphiniums are arranged among the other flowers.

This kind of attention to colour and contrast is all to be commended, but remember, as I mentioned before, when it comes to designing for a large space, like the barn, one must try not to get carried away with details at the expense of the overall scene. If it helps try and think of it as designing a stage set and use broad strokes to fill out the background, reserving the finer touches for the fore-

Though the dominant shades of harvest are warm yellow, gold and orange, the occasional introduction of a contrasting colour, as here in the cool white of the garlic and blue of the poppy heads and verticordia on the upper barrel, helps to sharpen and dramatize the main theme. The imaginative flower arranger is constantly experimenting with colour, adding muted shades to pretty pastels and looking for strong or subtle contrasts.

A perfect setting for a harvest supper, the table framed by the informal sweep of a hay garland

ground. Looking at the area in which we intended to site the supper table we realized that a large arrangement would be needed to fill the wall behind, and that something was required to link the beam over the table to everything going on beneath it.

Our solution for the wall was an arrangement of farm implements, wired together to make a rustic sculpture. This was based on a wooden backboard padded with moss and covered in chicken wire. We slung it on ropes over the beams, thus avoiding the use of screws or nails which might have damaged the fabric of the barn. Working *in situ* so that he could judge the best proportions and angles, it took Simon Lycett, one of a breed of new, young and necessarily athletic florists, only half an hour to attach the sieves, pitchforks, rakes and other implements using heavy gauge florists' wire. The outlines were softened with bunches of wheat while others, containing achillea, helichrysums, Chinese lanterns and phalaris, added colour.

For the beam above the table we made a hay garland. Of all the various forms of garland this is the quickest and easiest to make, requiring nothing more than a quantity of hay and plenty of thin silver reel wire. If you'd like to

make one yourself, start by taking a good handful of hay, teasing it out into a bulky rope and winding it with a spiral of reel wire. Position the loops of wire close enough together to hold the garland firmly, yet not so close that they become visible or make the garland too tight and rigid. Keep adding more handfuls of hay as you go along, easing out the rope shape and binding with wire. When you have the right length, tie the wire off tightly, then wind more of it back along the garland in the opposite direction.

This last step is important, as you'll discover if you should forget it. A hay garland is meant to be reasonably free and informal, but without a second strand of wire it will probably fall apart when you try to hang it up. No matter how well-made the garland, you may also find that it stretches, particularly if you attach anything to it. We fixed ours quite tightly, allowing for a few inches of droop when we added bunches of flowers to it. Our finished garland spiralled down the post supporting the beam, forming a frame for the table below.

The table itself is decorated with more bunches of helichrysums, sea lavender, bright yellow African daisies and golden broom bloom, tucked among the loaves that are displayed, appropriately enough, in old dough troughs. In the centre of the table is a low, mounded basket arrangement holding a combination of dried and seasonal fresh flowers. This is another version of the 'year-round' table arrangement which was invented, as its name suggests, to provide changing colour throughout the year. Basically it is a basket arrangement of sea lavender, alchemilla, nigella and white larkspur, flowers chosen for their variety of form and low-key colours that will complement a wide range of additions. To this basic arrangement may be added seasonal dried and fresh flowers to create an impressive display that's particularly useful as a centrepiece for a dining-table.

*Filling an awkward stretch of wall can be difficult. Here the problem is
solved with a collection of old agricultural tools hung together and
trimmed with dried flowers and wheat. These small touches demonstrate
how easy it is to bring colour and light to what could have been a lifeless
display. You can use the same technique to brighten your own home. Try
hanging a colourful tied bouquet from the end of a plain bedstead or a
cupboard doorhandle, or brighten a static collection of baskets, pottery
or copperware by adding simple bunches of home-dried garden flowers.*

*The harvest table, decorated with simple country bunches of wheat,
oats, gold and bronze helichrysums, sea lavender and yellow daisies. In
the centre of the table is the year-round arrangement, a combination of
dried and fresh flowers that can be varied throughout the year.*

There are two obvious advantages to this type of multi-purpose arrangement. First, it is quick and easy to use and doesn't require any great skill. One simply has to snip off the fresh flowers and insert them directly into the plastic foam base, where they will last for a day or two. Or, if you prefer, small plastic or glass florists' vials can be buried in the foam and filled with water. Fresh flowers placed in these will last much longer. Whichever technique you choose, it takes just a few minutes to create a densely-packed basket that looks as if hours have been spent on it.

Secondly, it's economical. In an ideal world no one would approach the subject of flowers with a budget in mind. The best arrangements, fresh or dried, are generous in scale and content and very often in expense, too. My business experience, however, has taught me that for most people cost is a significant factor. The joy of this arrangement is that a few fresh flowers go a long way and look surprisingly impressive. Using the dried material as a base, it's possible to have a large and eye-catching arrangement that changes its appearance from week to week and season to season, yet doesn't break the bank.

For the harvest festival table we added fresh trumpet-shaped orange alstroemeria and apricot spray chrysanthemums, and dried bracken and poppy heads, all of which gave a warm, autumnal feel. The alstroemeria and chrysanths were temporary additions, but there are other fresh flowers that once inserted into vials or foam will slowly dry out and become a permanent part of the arrangement. Hydrangeas, heather, statice, helichrysums and African proteas, among others, will all dry attractively if left in place. One word of warning. If you choose to use vials to hold the fresh flowers, fill them carefully and try not to get the dried flowers wet, otherwise they will rot.

Most of the arrangements and ideas we devised for the harvest festival can be adapted to suit other occasions, too. Though Thanksgiving is usually a more formal affair than a harvest supper, many of the arrangements you see on these pages can be easily adapted for a smarter interior setting. Take some of the simple bunches, for example, that decorate our table, and arrange them in a container – or hang one on a ribbon from the back of each chair around a dining-table. Take the hay garland (page 108), cover it with Chinese lanterns, small bunches of wheat and corn on the cob and drape it around a door or across the table. Instead of garlanding barrels or baskets, use flowers to decorate ceramic platters or bowls – the garlands can be held in place with tape and removed without damaging the container. A row of wheatsheaves in diminishing sizes ranged across a sideboard will look great. Or for something a little different, take the idea of the lavender arrangement on page 101 and adapt it, filling a simple Shaker-influenced wooden box with upright sprigs. Lavender is, in fact, an appropriate flower for Thanksgiving. It was the brightest colour that the Quakers were traditionally allowed to wear. In this way, developing your own associations and bringing your own ideas to bear, you can adapt almost all the arrangements to suit a specific occasion or a more formal style.

The barn would also make a wonderful setting for a summer party or barn dance, for example, and to ring the changes one doesn't have to do much more than change the colour scheme. For a midsummer night's celebration, shown on page 113, we chose zinging pink, red, yellow and blue that gave quite a different feel to the supper table.

The bunches arranged in the dough troughs were replaced with new ones containing oats, sea lavender, pink helichrysums and dark blue larkspur. A plain apple basket became a work of art, its handle bound with a moss garland covered in vivid red roses, yellow mimosa, delphiniums, alchemilla, touches of yellow achillea and bright orange gomphrenas. More gomphrenas were combined with yellow roses and blue delphiniums for bow-tied bunches at the sides.

A large platter-shaped basket full of strawberries was encircled with a garland that illustrates two separate moods. At the back, orange Chinese lanterns positively sizzle among delphiniums and red roses, very neatly illustrating my earlier point about how well complementary colours can set each other off. The other half of the garland is rather more subdued in colour, but attractive nevertheless. Yellow roses and achillea, pale delphiniums and nigella are offset by pink titree.

In the right-hand corner of the picture, completely transformed by the addition of fresh roses, sweet peas and foliage from the garden at Armscote, is the year-round table arrangement in a summery incarnation. It looks wonderful, and I am particularly pleased with the way in which the basic ingredients have accommodated such a major shift in colour. What better centrepiece could one ask for the perfect midsummer night's supper table?

Midsummer magic. Raspberries and strawberries were the inspiration for this midsummer night's variation on the harvest theme. Replace the warm golden tones of autumn with the sizzling colours on the summer garden and you have baskets and garlands so vibrant they almost dazzle the eye. In the corner, transformed with roses and sweet peas picked fresh from the gardens at Armscote, is the year-round table decoration in its midsummer finery.

Making the Arrangement

A YEAR-ROUND DECORATION

The year-round arrangement is designed for people who like their flowers to change from week to week and season to season. It is a basic basket loosely filled with low-key flowers that make a good background for the fresh and seasonal dried flowers that are added throughout the year. In designing it we originally intended it to make a useful centrepiece for a dining-table, but it could be used anywhere you need an unusual feature.

Fresh flowers can be added to the dry foam base, where they will last for a day or two, depending on variety. To make them last longer, you can insert a number of florists' vials into the foam and fill them with water using an eye dropper, or wrap the stems in damp moss and place the fresh flowers into them.

This arrangement has its advantages. It is constantly changing and so one never becomes bored with it (though of course you can always adapt dried-flower arrangements if you become tired of them). And with just a few fresh flowers you can very quickly achieve an impressive, colourful arrangement that would have required time and a large quantity of fresh material to produce from scratch.

MATERIALS REQUIRED
- *Medium-sized oval basket*
- *Dry foam blocks*
- *Scissors and a knife*
- *Stub wires*
- *Florists' vials (optional)*
- *Sea lavender, nigella, alchemilla, white larkspur*

1 Cut the dry foam blocks to size and secure them inside the basket using stub wires bent into a U-shape. If you wish to use plastic vials for holding the fresh flowers, it is best to insert them at random in the foam at this stage.

2 Take all the dried materials and cut and wire them into individual bunches by trimming the stems to within a few inches of the flower heads. (Further instructions for wiring bunches can be found on page 118.) Start inserting one variety at random.

3 Build up the arrangement using the other materials. In this case the basic flowers are nigella, sea lavender, alchemilla and white larkspur.

4 The finished arrangement is quite loose, to allow for the addition of fresh and seasonal material when required. It can be adapted to create an arrangement for Easter, Christmas, Autumn or Summer.

For Easter we chose to add brightly-coloured polyanthus to the basic arrangements, but there are innumerable alternatives for the early months of the year. Try hyacinths or narcissi for fragrance, scarlet tulips and golden daffodils for cheerful colour, amaryllis for drama or delicate apple and cherry blossom for a subtle, truly seasonal, appeal.

Oranges, holly and sprigs of yew were our Christmas additions, but they're not the only options. Spruce, pine cones and Christmas roses would give a more traditional effect: vibrant red poinsettias or rust-red chrysanthemums offer intense colour; and for fun one could insert Christmas tree baubles, tiny presents and touches of glitter.

For additional autumn colour we added orange alstroemeria and apricot-coloured chrysanthemums to the dried material. Other seasonal alternatives include dahlias, sedums, winter-flowering jasmine, passion flowers, blackberry brambles, sprigs of berry-covered pyracantha and autumn-tinted foliage.

The midsummer garden is so full of superb flowers that we were spoiled for choice! In the end we chose dazzling sweet peas and red spray roses, which both look and smell wonderful, to add to the basic arrangement. Scented stocks, cornflowers, sweet William, honeysuckle, jasmine, poppies, fresh alchemilla, lavender, gypsophila would all make truly delightful summer additions.

A COTSWOLD MANOR CHRISTMAS

Every old house has its own individual character, and for our Christmas setting we wanted to find somewhere we could decorate on a grand scale. A tall ceiling to accommodate a big Christmas tree and a large fireplace for an open log fire were the first two requirements on our list. We found these and many more delights at a manor house just a few miles from Armscote. Approached through apple orchards and an avenue of walnut trees, it has an imposing but friendly atmosphere. Its vast wood-panelled hall overlooked by an impressive gallery combines formality with a lived-in feel. This is the perfect home for a traditional Christmas.

Finding our location was one thing. Finding fresh ideas for the arrangements was something else entirely. Other books seem to skip over this difficult, head-scratching stage of the creative process and pretend that original ideas flow freely. I'd like to put the record straight. Occasionally one does have a blinding flash of insight, but most of the time it's just plain hard work that eventually results in a good idea. As usual when stuck for ideas we had a brainstorming session and asked ourselves what kind of themes we associated with Christmas.

Holly, ivy, mistletoe, Santa Claus, reindeer and pine cones immediately sprung to mind – nothing very original there. A partridge in a pear tree was a possibility, but how could we use the theme to decorate the whole hall? Christmas stockings seemed too naive for such a sophisticated setting, but the idea stuck with us. We thought a little harder. What does one find in a Christmas stocking? Oranges. This led to thoughts of mulled wine and the heady scent of oranges and cloves. And one just had to put oranges and cloves together to have the spicy, Christmassy fragrance of pomanders. At last we had our Christmas theme and one that was sharper and more sophisticated than the usual red, green and silver colour scheme, yet just as traditional in its own way and ideally suited to the character of our setting.

Oranges were also a good choice for another reason. When using flowers on a grand scale like this, it can help to include some large, bold materials that will add strong colour and drama to simple and relatively plain arrangements. In this way you can reduce the amount of detailed work required, a great saving on time and effort. By using oranges, tartan bows and bunches of small red glass baubles for our 'strokes' of bright colour, and a background of subdued dark greens and reds for the basic arrangements, we hoped to achieve a good contrast of depth and brightness.

It's a long haul from having the original ideas to realizing them, of course, and if you are embarking on a major series of arrangements I would strongly recommend you begin work on one of the smaller items. It's both physically and emotionally easier to solve any problems you encounter if you're working on a small scale. I know from experience how disheartening it is to have to 'unmake' a large arrangement. Once you've ironed out any unexpected hitches – colours not working as planned, awkward textures or unexpected effects – you can move on to the larger items.

Our troubleshooting arrangement was the wreath, shown on page 119. This was constructed on a commercial wire wreath frame that we covered with moss, bound in place with reel wire. The background material was spiky sea lavender, wired into place and then sprayed a dark, slightly glossy green using a paint gun. I use this method for many of the Christmas arrangements we make at

Armscote, and for several reasons. Sea lavender is cheap and easy to work with and, once sprayed, gives an excellent effect. The dark green paint is a more traditional and useful colour than some of the shades of dried foliage available. If you'd like to try out this idea yourself, you can do so by using aerosol paint to spray the sea lavender. Over this base we wired dark green kunzea, overlaid with bright green and deep red-brown amaranthus. To this were added knots of poppy seed heads and fir cones which can either be stuck in position or wired in place using heavy gauge stub wire.

If you decide to use wire for the fir cones, simply push one end of the wire through the lowest scales, circle it tightly around the cone and then twist the two ends together. Use scissors or wire cutters to trim the shorter end, if necessary, and use the longer one to attach the cone to the wreath.

To make the clusters of poppy seed heads or any other kind of flowers, take a small bunch of the material and cut the stems to within three inches (7.5cm) of the flower heads. Hold a stub wire vertically against the stems, aligning the end of the wire with them. With the other hand, take the wire round behind the stems about one inch (2.5cm) below the flower heads. Now twist the long end of the wire down round the stems in a spiral, covering the shorter end as you go. Use the long end of the wire as a stalk to stick into dry foam, or to bind the bunch tightly to a wreath or garland. Wiring a bunch is one of the fundamental techniques of dried-flower arranging, yet it's surprisingly difficult to master at first. Everyone seems to develop their own, highly individual, methods to make it easier, but it takes plenty of practice to discover them. It's worthwhile, however, as it enables you to achieve a thick, tight cluster of flowers on a single flexible stem which is far easier to work with than individual, brittle-stemmed flowers. Wired bunches can make all the difference to low,

dense arrangements which will look smooth and tightly-packed, with nothing visible but flower heads. Without them one tends to get a loosely filled arrangement through which stalks and too often patches of dry foam can be seen.

Returning to the next stage of our Christmas wreath, we added cinnamon sticks, wired in small bundles, and tartan bows to the fir cones, glass balls and poppy heads. The arrangement was made-up in advance and we added the satsumas at the last minute by simply piercing them with a long stub wire, twisting the ends together and using the long end to secure the fruit to the wreath. The smell was quite intoxicating and soon had everyone humming Christmas carols. Wired like this, fruit will last for at least a week before rotting, much longer if conditions are warm and dry enough for it to dry out. After Christmas the oranges, so long as they are not rotten, are quite safe to consume if the part through which the wire has passed is cut out.

Around the doorframe we hung a simple rope garland covered in kunzea, fern and sprigs of blue spruce and yew. The latter will dry extremely well if given a good spray of a fixative such as hair lacquer or one of the commercial products sold to prevent Christmas trees dropping their needles. The blue spruce of the garland ties in with the large, mounded arrangement on the circular table. This dense tapestry of colour and texture was made using kunzea and amaranthus, studded with bunches of blue-green and glowing red verticordia, dark brown oak leaves, fresh variegated holly, yew and masses of trailing ivy. Among this oranges, glass balls and fir cones contribute to the free, richly-coloured effect.

The fragrances of the oranges and
the pine needles combine in these
arrangements to create an
instantly festive mood

Its qualities are best appreciated from a short distance, as the picture on the previous two pages shows. Here one can appreciate the effect of all the arrangements together. I must say that it really was a spellbinding scene; the kind of Christmas setting one dreams of but doesn't expect to see. It is difficult to know quite where to begin describing it, but I should perhaps start at the fireplace which we draped with another length of rope garland wired with oranges and satsumas. I draw your attention to this because I am always nervous of using dried flowers near candles and fires. One can minimize the risks by applying a flame-proofing spray to the arrangements, but I have seen for myself how quickly dried flowers can catch light and I would still urge caution.

Caution was not in evidence, however, when we decorated the magnificent Christmas tree. Here I must thank my great friend Hamish Greycheap, who supplied it at such short notice. We covered this splendid specimen with decorations, many of them containing dried flowers. Particularly attractive are the small red and green cane wreaths, each with a spray of flowers. Should you feel that we have cheated by using a fresh Christmas tree for our pictures, turn to page 126 and you'll find illustrated instructions on how to make one from dried foliage and flowers. Unfortunately six feet is about the height limit; after that one requires such large branches of dried material that their weight becomes too much to deal with. If you have a room as large as the one seen here, I'm afraid there is no option but to choose a fresh Christmas tree.

Dried flowers provide the backdrop for a classic Christmas Eve scene. There are presents around the tree, chestnuts in a basket by the fire, candles flickering on the mantelpiece and, no doubt, carol singers outside the front door.

On the table in front of the tree is the familiar shape of the year-round centrepiece arrangement (described in detail on page 114). For its Christmas appearance it strikes a suitably festive note, studded with oranges and covered with sprigs of holly and yew. Yew berries are both poisonous and extremely attractive to children, so take great care when including them in an arrangement and be prepared to omit them if necessary.

Another arrangement full of seasonal materials is the garden trug at the foot of the chair. It contains walnuts gathered from the trees that line the approach to this house and is decorated very simply with fir cones and long cinnamon sticks. The cones have been scented with a few drops of spicy essential oil so that they release a rich fragrance which combines well with the sharpness of the oranges.

The fruit-filled basket placed on the table with its delightfully fragrant pomanders, adds to the heady atmosphere of the room. Though they're wonderful to have around the house at any time of year, pomanders have always been associated with Christmas and make wonderful decorations. To make pomanders yourself you will need firm, unblemished oranges or apples, a good store of high-quality, large-headed cloves and a thick darning needle for piercing holes.

Make holes at regular intervals all over the fruit, inserting the cloves as you go. Leave a gap of about a quarter of an inch (0.6cm) between the cloves so that the skin doesn't split. If you intend to hang the pomander on a ribbon, leave a clove-free channel, half an inch wide (1.2cm), around its middle. This will hold the ribbon neatly in place. To prevent the pomanders from rotting they must be 'cured' in a spice mixture for a period of two weeks or more. The following recipe will give enough of the mixture to cure several pomanders at once. It can be re-used many times. In a large bowl mix together the following

ingredients: 2oz (50g) of powdered cloves, 4oz (100g) of powdered cinnamon, 1 dessertspoon of powdered nutmeg, 1 dessertspoon of powdered allspice and 1oz (25g) of powdered orrisroot. Place the pomanders in this mixture and turn them gently so that they are completely covered. Continue to turn them each day, ensuring they are well dusted with spices, until they are hard and shrunken. Remove them from the mixture, dust them off and use them as you like. Piled in a bowl in the living-room or hanging in a wardrobe, they will perfume the air with a rich, spicy but fresh scent that everyone will appreciate. Pomander-making is the kind of task that children enjoy, and the fruits of their labours, if they can bear to part with them, make very acceptable presents. Next time they complain that they have nothing to do, why not sit them down with oranges, cloves and small knitting needles and introduce them to this ancient art?

When we were planning our arrangements for the gallery we considered making bunches of ribboned pomanders and hanging them from the broad posts spaced along it at intervals. Eventually this idea was dropped in

The gallery. Seen from straight on, the orange trees and central swag of the garland frame the tapestry, creating a pleasing symmetry. Arrangements like these take time to make, but when you have a feature worth highlighting, such as this, they're worth it. Once made, they can be used for several years, and by varying their contents they can be brought out for occasions other than Christmas. Remove the oranges, cones, ribbons and glass baubles and replace them with roses, lavender, white larkspur and blue delphiniums, for example, and you have beautiful arrangements for a wedding or a party.

favour of the solution you can see on the previous page. Three broad garlands containing our key materials — oranges, fir cones, ribbons, poppy heads and shining red baubles — were suspended across the balustrade. Because the central span was wider than those on either side we deliberately gave the middle garland a deeper drop. The width of its span just happened to be the same as the width of the beautiful old tapestry that hangs on the gallery wall. As if the combination of these two elements wasn't enough, we topped each of the gallery's main posts with an orange tree to create a frame for the tapestry. The symmetry of this design suited the formality of the hall, once again illustrating the importance of using flowers that complement the character of the setting.

We measured the required length of garland, as on previous occasions using a rope, and like the broad garland in the church, it was made using moss-filled chicken wire. Before we began adding the flowers and foliage we marked its centre. Then we began working at each end and moved inwards towards the centre. This is a point worth remembering if your material has a definite direction and you want a symmetrical look to the finished arrangement. Our materials for the garlands and the orange trees were the same as those for the wreath, green-sprayed sea lavender with kunzea and two different colours of amaranthus.

All the arrangements on these pages can be stored and re-used year after year, so none of the trouble (and pleasure) of making them is wasted. Perishable material such as the oranges should be removed before the arrangements are put away in boxes at the end of the season. Store them in a dry place and, if you can obtain them, add a sachet or two of silica gel to the boxes before they are closed (see page 132). These will absorb any excess moisture in the air and ensure that the dried material stays dry. Each year you can ring the changes by adding new and different touches to the basic garlands. For example, small Christmas crackers and gift-wrapped parcels could be wired in for a brighter effect; Chinese lanterns and gold-sprayed cones would give a cheerful yet subtle display; or you could look around your home and locality for your own sources of inspiration.

If you find the prospect of making garlands and Christmas trees a daunting one, then you may be reassured to know that there are other, simpler, arrangements at the opposite end of the scale. As the picture on the right shows, even the smallest of dried-flower bunches has its uses at Christmas. We used tiny off cuts of white gypsophila, each trimmed with a green leaf, some red glixia and a ribbon, to decorate the branches of the Christmas tree. Other tree arrangements include tiny cane wreaths, available from all good dried-flower supply shops (see page 135), spray-painted red and green and decorated with a few strands of sea lavender, a helichrysum and a small cone. These can be used to decorate not just the tree but the gifts around it. Other trimmings for special Christmas presents include large fir cones decorated with spirals of ribbon, strands of moss and an assortment of berries and flowers. Small decorations like this are an ideal way of using up the odd flowers and leaves left when you have finished a larger arrangement and provide the finishing touch to any gift.

The finishing touch to Christmas presents. Tiny bunches of dried flowers, made from off cuts from previous arrangements, are tied with ribbon or added to small cane rings to make gift trimmings. Pine cones too large to be hung from the tree or used in arrangements are decorated with moss, ribbon, berries and flowers to make spectacular gift tags.

Making the Arrangement

A CHRISTMAS TREE

A dried-flower Christmas tree makes a practical and attractive alternative to the real thing. It's far nicer to have around than a plastic tree, it doesn't shed its needles, and it can be put away on Twelfth Night and saved for the following year.

At Armscote we make thousands of Christmas trees of all shapes and sizes each year. One of our methods for the smaller trees is to use spiky sea lavender as the basic foliage. Once the tree has been covered with it, the whole thing is spray-painted a dark, faintly glossy green. We use a paint gun but aerosol paint is just as good. The result is excellent.

For larger trees one needs larger materials and the idea of spraying becomes less practical. The basic foliage of the tree shown here is dark green kunzea, but there are various alternatives available. Yew and spruce also dry well and would make very appropriate foliage.

I would advise strongly against using lights on this type of tree. Even though dried material can be sprayed with a flame retardant to make it fireproof, I think it is an unnecessary risk. And bear in mind that because the tree isn't very strong, any decorations you hang from it should be fairly lightweight.

The finished Christmas tree, complete with garland

MATERIALS REQUIRED

- *Large terracotta pot*
- *Sharpened branch*
- *16 four-inch nails and hammer*
- *Thistle plaster*
- *Expanded polystyrene packaging bubbles*
- *Dry foam blocks and cone*
- *Scissors and a knife*
- *Tape*
- *Stub and reel wires*
- *Ribbon and trimmings*
- *Kunzea, orsparsa, white titree, bupleurum, sphagnum moss, forest moss, reindeer moss, fir cones, gypsophila, glixia, Nigella orientalis*

1 Sharpen one end of a large branch, hammer in 16 large nails, as shown in the picture, and set the branch in thistle plaster (see page 69). Impale blocks of dry foam on the nails.

2 Attach a foam cone on the top of the branch. Use glue and tape, if necessary, to hold all the foam firm. Outline the shape of the tree by adding the basic foliage.

3 Continue to add the green foliage and highlight here and there with clusters of white. I used bupleurum and white titree, both of which have solid, woody stems that can be easily inserted into the foam. Finish the pot with a layer of sphagnum moss.

4 When the tree is ready, make a garland for it. A dried tree becomes less of a fake and more of a concept if decorated with dried materials. Use grey forest moss and bind it into a garland with reel wire. Wind tartan ribbon round it. We also added a long string of shiny red beads, available from the haberdashery departments of most stores.

5 Wire together tiny bunches of flowers – I used bleached gypsophila and red glixia, finished with a seed head of Nigella orientalis. Conceal the wire with a ribbon and add each bunch to the garland.

6 Add the finishing touches – pieces of dyed, light green reindeer moss, secured with a short U-shaped wire and white-sprayed fir cones.

CHAPTER FIVE

A
RESOURCE
GUIDE

If the previous chapters of this book have inspired you to dry your own flowers, or make your own arrangements, you'll find this section useful. It contains practical information on methods of drying a wide range of material at home, on suppliers of dried flowers, on the tools of the trade and on plant names, which often cause confusion. Like all arts, arranging dried flowers has to be practised to be learned. I hope this information will make the learning process easier — and I hope that, like me, you will discover in dried flowers a source of great pleasure and self-expression.

Some of the wide selection of materials and accessories available at the Armscote Manor shop. Though there is an extensive range of flower-arranging equipment on the market, beginners need only a basic kit of florists' scissors, a long-bladed knife, stub wires and dry foam to get started.

DRYING YOUR OWN FLOWERS

There are various methods of drying flowers, some more suited to certain types of material than others. But before describing the processes, a few words on picking your own flowers for drying. Most flowers, particularly roses and peonies, are best picked just before they come into full bloom. Don't wait until they are fully open. If you do, they will shed their petals as they dry. Pick only the best flowers and ignore any that are diseased or badly blemished. It is best to harvest them in fine weather, not when they are still damp from rain or dew, and hang them as soon as possible.

Air Drying

Air drying is the simplest and most common means of preserving flowers and other types of plant material. When we grew and dried large quantities of material at Armscote in the early days of the business, it was the main method of preservation we used. I still air dry flowers cut from the garden, either in our kitchen or in the loft space above the work-room.

The main requirement for this process is a warm, dry area with plenty of circulating air. If it's dark, too, it will help preserve the colour of the flowers. Don't hang flowers where they will be in direct sunlight. During the summer a loft makes an ideal hanging place. Failing this a dry garage or shed, a spare room, a boiler room or an airing cupboard will do. The temperature should be a minimum 10°C, 50°F.

When you have found a suitable place and cut your flowers, remove the lower leaves and tie the material into manageable bunches – four or five stems is enough for most plants. I find rubber bands useful for holding bunches together. They grip the stems as they dry out and shrink. If you are using twine, bind the bunches tightly or stems may fall to the floor when dry. Large flowers and seed heads (artichokes and onion heads, for example) and plants with dense foliage should be strung individually. Most material can then be simply hung upside down from nails or a line, or on a rack – an old clothes horse is ideal – to dry. Don't hang the bunches too closely together or overload the space. Air must be able to circulate around and between the material so that moisture can evaporate. Large-headed material, including artichokes and maize, can be laid out to dry on sheets of newspaper or on a layer of chicken wire stretched over a fruit box. Stick the stems through the chicken wire so that the heads dry in an upright position.

In my experience almost all flowers and plants can be air dried, even delicate material such as daffodils. Experiment with the contents of your garden and see what happens. The very worst is that the petals will drop off – not much of a loss if one remembers that the flower would have died anyway.

Moss and lichen should also be dried by this method. Place them in a loose single layer in a wooden fruit box or lay them out on sheets of crumpled newspaper. Don't pack them tightly or they will rot.

You can tell your flowers are dry when they become papery and their stems have shrunk. The process can take from between a week to a month or longer, depending on the materials and the conditions in which they are kept. The bigger, fleshier and more dense the material – artichokes and onion heads, for example – the slower the process. Don't be tempted to save time by taking flowers down before they are completely dry. Petals will fall out and the whole stem may begin to rot.

Some flowers will do better if the air drying process is started while they are in water – a contradictory but successful method. Hydrangeas, gypsophila, proteas, statice, mimosa and achillea all dry well if they are put upright in half an inch of water and then placed in the drying area. By the time the water has been absorbed, the flowers are likely to be dry.

Glycerine

I use glycerine for preserving foliage. I like to have a good supply of preserved ivy, beech and oak leaves throughout the year and this is the best way of keeping them. Like air drying, the basic technique is quite simple if you have the space and time to do it properly.

Mix two measures of hot water with one measure of glycerine and add a few inches of this concoction to a tall container. Take freshly cut branches or strands of ivy and place the cut ends in it. They will absorb it and become preserved in the process. Top up the container as required. As the glycerine is absorbed and rises through the twigs and leaves, you may be able to observe their gradual change in colour. When all the leaves have undergone this change you can remove the branch and use it in your arrangements. The length of time this process takes depends very much on the type of material you are drying. To speed it up and generally improve absorption, crush woody stems or cut them at an acute angle before inserting them into the glycerine mixture.

As for suitable materials, I make a practice of regularly experimenting with new types of foliage. Catkins, old man's beard, ferns, eucalyptus, pin oak, smoke bush, magnolia, laurel and indeed, the foliage of many common trees and shrubs can be preserved by this method. There are just a couple of points to note before embarking on the process for yourself. Always use fresh-cut branches and stems, which absorb the glycerine mixture more quickly and efficiently than old, half-dead material. Cut the stems when the sap is still rising, usually in the summer, and remove any damaged or new leaves before the glycerine reaches them as they don't respond well to it. Finally, a warning that this method can become surprisingly expensive. Start with just a few stems of foliage in a small container and see for yourself how much of the glycerine and water mix they absorb. Better by far to have one or two stems of perfectly preserved leaves than a bucketful of half-finished ones.

The wonderful thing about glycerined foliage is that it retains its suppleness, unlike flowers dried by other methods. Less pleasing, perhaps, is the change of colour that often results. Some foliage, particularly that with a naturally brown tint such as oak and copper beech, becomes a superb dark or bronzy brown, but green leaves may turn to a murky khaki and ivy occasionally yellows. To counteract this you can add a few drops of food colouring to the glycerine, which opens up all kinds of opportunities for unusual shades and variations.

To preserve individual large leaves or small sprays of leaves in glycerine, immerse them completely until their colour changes. Wash them in a mild detergent before using them in arrangements.

Desiccation

Another drying method which offers quite different results is desiccation. This is a time-consuming process best-suited to small quantities of flowers; I have rarely used it at Armscote because it is too labour intensive and expensive for use on a large scale. The process involves the use of a drying agent, usually silica gel, to absorb the water in the flowers and leave it perfectly dried. The results can be quite spectacular and it is possible to preserve both the colour and shape of delicate flowers such as tulips, lilies, orchids, anemones and daffodils almost perfectly. Other flowers, particularly the larger ones, suffer some discolouration, but are still useful for their dramatic size and form.

It would take time and dedication to dry sufficient quantities of flowers for a decent-sized arrangement. And because only the flower heads themselves are dried, one has to wire each of them up individually. I have seen air-dried arrangements featuring a few of these perfectly preserved flowers as a highlight, but can't personally recommend this approach. Neither type of material looked its best; the air-dried material seemed unduly dull and the desiccated flowers insubstantial and brittle against their robust background. However, desiccated flowers do look good when placed in bowls of potpourri or when arranged together to give an almost lifelike effect.

If you have the patience to try this method yourself you will need silica gel crystals. (Alum, borax and hot sand can all be used in the same way but take longer to work.) Silica crystals can be obtained from good florists' suppliers (see page 135) and from chemists. If there is a choice, buy the colour-indicator type. This will probably be a strong blue colour which will turn pink when it becomes moist, or white with blue grains which will change colour when they are damp. If necessary, grind the crystals in a food processor until they are the texture of fine-ground coffee. Take an airtight container – a biscuit tin or plastic food container is fine – and cover the base with a layer of the silica. Onto this place individual flower heads. They should not touch, so don't aim to pack in more than four or five medium-sized flowers.

Using an artist's paintbrush, ease the crystals between the petals. Slowly and carefully, so as not to distort the shape of the flowers, cover them completely with more of the silica. Seal the lid of the container and leave it for two days. When you open it after that time you may find that the crystals have changed colour. Excavate the flowers very gently using a slotted kitchen spoon. They should feel firm and dry. If they don't, put them back and test again the following day. Don't leave them longer than this before testing them because they will continue to dry out and will become increasingly brittle and difficult to handle. When they are dry, dust off any excess silica crystals using the paintbrush, and you should have a perfectly preserved and gorgeously-coloured flower to contribute to your arrangement. The silica crystals can be dried out in an oven and used for the next batch of flowers. Be very careful to keep these flowers in a warm, dry atmosphere, otherwise they may become limp and begin to wilt.

Some authorities suggest using this process for delphiniums, larkspur and roses, but personally I think these can be perfectly well air-dried. Air-dried roses may not look quite so lifelike in their bunches, but once steamed and opened individually they are superb. I would reserve the silica method for flowers that really can't be preserved in any other way.

If you have no immediate use for the flowers you have dried, store them in a cool, dry, airy place. They can be left hanging in their original bunches or put in boxes. Use newspaper or tissue paper to protect the flower heads and leave the top of the box open so that air can reach the material. Don't pack any flowers that are not completely dry – they may rot and ruin everything around them. Another potential storage problem worth mentioning is mice. Before you store your materials in a garage or shed, particularly in the country, make sure you don't have mice in there. They love dried flowers and can wreak absolute havoc with your precious materials.

Plants Suitable For Preserving With Glycerine

This list includes only those plants for which this method of preservation is the best option. Others, such as hydrangeas, may also be preserved in this way but are more easily air dried. This is by no means a comprehensive list, so don't feel nervous about experimenting with material from your garden.

Aspidistra leaves

Beech leaves

Bergenia

Box

Camellia leaves

Catkins

Chestnut leaves

Cotoneaster

Eleagnus

Eucalyptus leaves

Fatsia (preserve single leaves only)

Hypericum ferns

Ivy

Laurel leaves

Magnolia leaves

Mahonia

Mexican orange

Moluccella

Oak leaves

Rhododendron (preserve single leaves only)

Flowers Suitable For Desiccation

Almost all flowers are suited to this means of preservation, but it is most practical to concentrate on those delicate varieties that cannot be dried in any other way. Experiment and see what happens. If petals drop from flowers preserved in this way you can stick them back with a discreet spot of glue.

Anemone

Camellia

Carnations

Clematis

Cyclamen

Dahlia

Freesia

Gentian

Hellebore

Hyacinth

Iris

Lily flowers of all varieties

Marigold

Narcissus

Orchid

Pansy

Passion Flower

Poppy

Primrose

Rhododendron

Tulip

Violet

Wallflower

EQUIPMENT AND MATERIALS

The materials and implements used throughout this book are all obtainable from good florists' shops or suppliers (see page 135). To produce most of the arrangements one would need a basic kit consisting of:

Florists' scissors – strong, high-quality scissors for cutting plant stems and wires.

Stub/florists' wires – range in length from 3½-18 inches (9-37cm) and from fine to heavy gauge, 24 gauge to 18 gauge. The finer the gauge, the higher the number. Most professional florists use medium and heavy gauge wires, though they may be too tough for unskilled fingers to manipulate. The best length to begin with is around 9 inches (22.5cm).

Reel wire – comes in either silver or dark green. The dark green shows up less in arrangements. I recommend using 26 gauge.

Dry foam – looks similar to styrofoam, but is softer and holds flowers better. It can be bought in a variety of shapes and sizes. Unless you need a sphere or a cone, buy large blocks and cut them to size.

Carving/floral knife – or other long-bladed knife for cutting foam.

Other useful items of equipment include:

Florists' tape – narrow, shiny black on one side. It sticks well to dry foam and is useful for holding it in position.

Chicken wire – for creating a base for flowers. 1½ inch (3.5cm) gauge is the easiest to work with.

Gutta-percha/floral tape – a rubber-based tape used for winding around stem wires and concealing unattractive ends. It comes in a variety of shades.

Florists' spikes and dry foam fixative/setting clay – used together to secure dry foam to shallow bowls and other 'difficult' containers. A small piece of fixative/setting clay holds the spike to the container, and the dry foam is impaled on the spike. The fixative/setting clay can often be removed from glass and china containers without causing damage.

Glue – useful for sticking awkward flowers and materials to arrangements. Use fast-drying clear glue or, for stronger bonding, a glue gun.

Wreath rings and posy holders – useful commercially-available bases for wreaths and posies. They can save time and trouble and give neater results. Wire wreath rings are particularly useful because of their light weight.

SUPPLIERS OF DRIED FLOWERS

There are hundreds of dried-flower stockists all over the country. Look in the Yellow Pages directory under Florists and Florists' Supplies for an indication of those in your area. Many florists specify in their advertisements whether or not they sell dried flowers loose or arranged. It's also worth checking your local garden centre – an increasing number are offering dried material. Here are some further suggestions:

*All suppliers that are marked with this symbol stock Armscote Manor Dried Flowers' arrangements at the time of writing.

UK SUPPLIERS

In London:

Covent Garden Flower Market
New Covent Garden
London SW8
Tel: (01) 720 2211
The stockist I recommend here is Multiflora, which supplies many retailers and also sells flowers to the public – though you may have to buy some things in bulk rather than in individual bunches. They carry a comprehensive and ever-changing range of stock. If you plan to visit Covent Garden, go early. By 7.30-8 a.m. the market is beginning to close down.

James Bodenham & Co*
89 Jermyn Street
London SW1
Tel: (01) 930 5340

Chattels
53 Chalk Farm Road
London NW1
Tel: (01) 267 0877

Fenwicks of Bond Street*
63 New Bond Street
London W1
Tel: (01) 629 9161

General Trading Company
144 Sloane Street
London SW1
Tel: (01) 730 0411

Graham and Green*
4-7 Elgin Crescent
London W11
Tel: (01) 727 4594

Harrods Ltd*
Knightsbridge
London SW1
Tel: (01) 730 1234

Heal & Son Ltd
196 Tottenham Court Road
London W1
Tel: (01) 636 1666

Camilla Hepper*
296 Chiswick High Road
London W4
Tel: (01) 995 2293

Hillier & Hilton
98 Church Road
London SW13
Tel: (01) 748 1810

Longmans Florists*
Selfridges Ltd
Oxford Street
London W1
Tel: (01) 629 1234

and

46 Holborn Viaduct*
London EC1
Tel: (01) 583 1440

Westminster Cathedral Shop*
42 Francis St
London SW1
Tel: (01) 828 4962

The following two florists sell or can be commissioned to make arrangements of the very highest quality:

Robert Day Flowers
89 Pimlico Road
London SW1
Tel: (01) 824 8655

Kenneth Turner Flowers
35 Brook Street
London W1
Tel: (01) 629 7837

Stores with branches around the country selling loose dried flowers and/or arrangements include:

Boots*
Habitat – who also have a good variety of containers.
Homebase*
Lewis's*
Makro*
The National Trust*
Next
Perrings*

The following shops, listed alphabetically according to town or city, stock dried flowers and/or dried-flower arrangements. If you have precise requirements, telephone first and find out whether they can supply you.

Nova
20 Chapel Street
Aberdeen AB1 15P
Tel: (0224) 641270

Spats
97 Groomsport Road
Bangor
Northern Ireland
Tel: (0247) 453264

Talbot Gray Ltd
26 Horsemarket
Barnard Castle
County Durham DL12 8LZ
Tel: (0833) 38072

Temptation
211 High Street
Berkhamsted
Hertfordshire HP4 1AD
Tel: (0442) 874333

The Molescraft Garden Centre
114 Woodhall Way
Beverley
Yorkshire
Tel: (0482) 881172

China Plus
148 High Street
Chipping Ongar
Essex
Tel: (0277) 656178

Artworks
The Watershed
Canons Road
Bristol BS1 5UN
Tel: (0272) 294803

Trevor Edwards Garden Centre
Scotch Quarter
Carrickfergus
County Antrim
Northern Ireland
Tel: (09603) 51123

Grosvenor Garden Centre
Wrexham Road
Belgrave
Chester CH4 9EB
Tel: (0244) 682856

Dixon & Co
Church Street
Coleraine BT52 1A4
Northern Ireland
Tel: (0265) 42076

The Thursday Shop
52 Finkle Street
Cottingham
North Humberside HU16 4A2
Tel: (0482) 844921

The Dartington Trading Co. Ltd
Shinners Bridge
Dartington
Devon TQ9 6TQ
Tel: (0803) 864171

The Old Stockhouse
60 West Street
Dorking
Surrey RH4 1BS
Tel: (0306) 882783

Casa Fina
107 Hanover Street
Edinburgh EH1 2DJ
Tel: (031) 225 2442

Jenners
48 Princes Street
Edinburgh EH2 2YJ
Tel: (031) 225 2442

Ditman and Malpass
9 West Street
Havant
Hampshire DO9 1EN
Tel: (0705) 483047

First Base
11 Silver Walk
St Martins Square
Leicester LE1 5EW
Tel: (0533) 629215

Jasmin
Holly Court
118 High Street
Midsomer Norton
Avon BA3 2DL
Tel: (0761) 419202

Country Choice
2 Blenheim Road
Minehead
Somerset TA24 5PY
Tel: (0643) 706584

Barkers
198-202 High Street
Northallerton
North Yorkshire DL7 8LP
Tel: (0609) 772303

Hovells
Bridewell Alley
Norwich NR2 1AE
Tel: (0603) 626676

Campion
26 High Street
Uppermill
Oldham
Lancashire
Tel: (0457) 876341

Pickwick Papers
The Gallery
90 Gloucester Green
Oxford OX1 2BU
Tel: (0865) 793149

J.R. Taylor
4-12 Garden Street
St Annes-on-Sea
Lancashire FY8 2AB
Tel: (0253) 722266

Clouds of Swansea
Unit 8
St David's Centre
Swansea SA1 3LE
Tel: (0792) 648093

Armscote Manor Dried Flowers
Armscote
Near Stratford-upon-Avon
Warwickshire CV37 8DA
Tel: (060882) 681

Mc'Illroy's
64-72 Regent Street
Swindon
Wiltshire SN1 1JX
Tel: (0793) 619487

US SUPPLIERS

Arrowhead Gardens
115 Boston Post Road
Wayland, MA 01778
Tel: (508) 358-7333

Bachman's Inc
6010 Lyndale Avenue South
Minneapolis, MN 55419
Tel: (612) 861-7600

W. Atlee Burpee Co
300 Park Avenue
Warminster, PA 18974
Tel: (215) 674-4900

Carroll Gardens
P.O. Box 310
Westminster, MD 21157
Tel: (301) 848-5422
(Sell flower-drying kits)

Emlong Nurseries
2671 West Marquette Woods Road
Stevensville, MI 49127
Tel: (616) 429-3431

Farmer Seed and Nursery
818 Northwest 4th Street
Faribault, MN 55021
Tel: (507) 334-1625

Earl Ferris Nursery
811 4th Street, NE
Hampton, IA 50441
Tel: (515) 456 2563

Sjulin's Swedish Touch
RR2, Box 2
Hamburg, IA 51640
Tel: (712) 382-2383

Jung Seed Co
335 South High Street
Randolph, W1 53957
Tel: (414) 326-3121

Keil Brothers
220-15 Horace Harding Blvd.
Bayside, NY 11364
Tel: (718) 224-2020

Moon Mountain Wildflowers
P.O. Box 34
Morro Bay, CA 93442
Tel: (805) 772-2473

L.L. Olds Seeds Co
2901 Packers Avenue
Madison, W1 53704
Tel: (608) 249-9291

Putney Nursery
Box 265
Putney, VT 05340
Tel: (802) 387-5577

Scarff's Nursery
Route 1
Carlisle, OH 45344
Tel: (513) 845-3130

People's Flower Corporation
786 6th Avenue
New York, NY 10001
Tel: (212) 686-6291

Rialto Florist, Inc
707 Lexington Ave
New York, NY 10022
Tel: (212) 688-3204

Richard Salome Flowers
152 East 79th St
New York, NY 10021
Tel: (212) 988-2933

Smith & Hawken
23 Corte Madera
Mill Valley, CA 94941
Tel: (415) 383-4050

Galerie Felix Flower
968 Lexington Ave
New York, NY 10021
Tel: (212) 772-7701

Gardener's Eden
Williams Sonoma
P.O. Box 7307
San Francisco, CA 91120
Tel: (415) 421-4242

The following suppliers ship dried plants to order:

Catnip Acres Herb Nursery
67 Christian Street
Oxford, Connecticut 06483
Tel: (203) 885-5649
(Dried flowers and herbs. Seed catalogue $2.)

Stamens & Pistils
875 Third Avenue
New York, NY 10022
Tel: (212) 593-1888
(Dried tropical flowers and foliage. No catalogue.)

Sura Kayla
484 Broome Street
New York, NY 10013
Tel: (212) 941-8757
(Dried flowers and grasses. For brochure send SASE.)

Tom Thumb Workshop
Route 13
P.O. Box 357
Mappsville, VA 23407
Tel: (804) 824-3507
(Dried flowers and herbs. Catalogue $1.)

Wayside Gardens
1 Garden Lane
Hodges, SC 29695-0001
Tel: (800) 845-1124
(Dried flowers. Free catalogue.)

Well-Sweep Herb Farm
317 Mount Bethel Road
Port Murray, NJ 07865
Tel: (201) 852-5390
(Dried flowers and herbs. Catalogue $1.)

A PLANT LEXICON

Identifying plants can be a confusing business. All have Latin names, which it can be useful to know when ordering flowers from suppliers or buying seed to grow in the garden. Many plants are known by the abbreviated version of the Latin name, for example, *Alchemilla mollis* is usually known as alchemilla – and, then again, it's sometimes called by its traditional name, Lady's mantle. To complicate things further not all authorities agree on all the names. Where there is doubt, I have used the name by which we buy and sell the flowers at Armscote Manor.

In the table below I have listed the names of the most commonly available dried flowers. There simply isn't space to list every one of the different varieties of some species – one could write a short book on the different banksias and proteas alone – so I suggest you visit or contact suppliers in order to see for yourself what they have on offer.

Those plants which can fairly easily be grown in temperate climates and will make an attractive contribution to the flowerbeds I have marked with this symbol*. If you live in an area with a more extreme climate, consult an appropriate gardening book.

Latin Name	Common Name	Traditional Name
Acacia sp.	Mimosa/wattle	
Acanthus spinosus*	Acanthus	Bear's breeches
Achillea filipendulina*	Achillea	Yarrow
Achillea millefolium*	Lilac achillea	Yarrow
Achillea ptarmica	Achillea ptarmica	The Pearl/Pearl Achillea
Aconitum napellus*	Aconitum	Monkshood
Agapanthus africanus*	Agapanthus (seed heads)	
Agonis sp.	Titree	
Agrostis nebulosa	Cloud grass	
Alchemilla mollis*	Alchemilla	Lady's mantle
Allium sp.*	Onion	
Amaranthus sp.*	Amaranthus	Love-lies-bleeding/Prince's feathers
Ambrosinia sp.	Ambrosinia	
Ammobium alatum*	Sandflower	Winged flower
Anaphalis sp.*	Pearl everlasting	
Anethum graveolens*	Dill	
Anigozanthos sp.	Kangaroo paw	
Aphyllanthes sp.	Glixia	Grass daisy
Arctosis sp.	African daisy	
Artemisia vulgaris*	Artemisia	Mugwort
Arundinaria sp.*	Bamboo	
Astilbe davidii*	Astilbe	
Avena compacta*	Oats	
Banksia sp.	Banksia	Australian honeysuckle
Bergenia sp.*	Bergenia	Elephant's ear
Betula pendula	Silver birch	
Botao branco	Botao	Button flower
Briza maxima*	Large quaking grass	Pearl grass
Briza media*	Common quaking grass	
Briza minima*	Lesser quaking grass	
Briza segromi	Briza segromi	
Bromus formus	Bromus	Spear grass
Bupleurum sp.	Bupleurum	Gloss eyes
Buxifolium sp.	Buxifolium	
Calendula officinalis*	Pot marigold	
Callistemon beaufortia sparsa*	Red bottlebrush	
Capucin sp.	Capucin	
Carex sp.	Sedge	Bell reed
Carlina acaulis*	Stemless thistle	
Carthamus tinctorius*	Carthamus	Safflower or saffron thistle
Caspium limonium*	Caspia	
Caustus sp.	Caustus	Chinese puzzle
Celosia argentea cristata	Celosia	Cockscomb
Centaurea cyanus*	Cornflower	
Choisya ternata*	Choisya	Mexican orange blossom
Chrysanthemum sp.*	Chrysanthemum	
Chrysanthemum vulgare*	Tansy	
Cladonia sp.	Lichen	Reindeer or staghorn moss
Clematis vitalba*	Wild clematis	Old man's beard, Travellers' joy
Cortaderia selloana*	Pampas grass	
Craspedia globosa*	Craspedia	Drumstick plant
Cynara scolymus*	Globe artichoke	

Dahlia*	Pompon dahlia	
Delphinium consolida*	Larkspur	
Delphinium sp.*	Delphinium	
Dryandra formosa	Dryandra	
Dryopteris filix-mas*	Male fern	
Dudinea sp.	Dudinea	
Dumosa limonium iertericum*	Statice dumosa	Sea Lavender
Echinops ritro*	Miniature thistle	
Echinops bannaticus*	Globe thistle	
Erica cinerea*	Bell heather	
Eryngium planum*	Sea holly	
Eucalyptus sp.	Eucalyptus	Gum
Fagus sylvatica*	Beech	
Fagus sylvatica 'Cuprea'*	Copper beech	
Gomphrena globosa*	Globe amaranth	Spanish clover
Gossypium herbaceum	Cotton	
Grimmia pulvinata	Bun moss	
Gypsophila sp.*	Gypsophila	Baby's breath
Gypsophila rugosa	Broom bloom	
Hakea cucallata	Hakea	
Hedera helix*	Ivy	
Helichrysum angustifolium*	Curry plant	Stinking helichrysum
Helichrysum bracteatum*	Helichrysum	Everlasting flower/ strawflower
Helichrysum cordatum*	Seacrest	
Helichrysum sesamoides*	Helichrysum	Everlasting flower
Helichrysum vestitum	Capblumen	
Helipterum manglesii	Rhodante	
Helipterum sanfordii	Cluster-flowered everlasting	
Helipterum sp.*	Acroclinium	
Helipterum subufolium	Helipterum	Sunray
Hordeum vulgare	Barley	
Humulus lupulus*	Hop	
Hydrangea macrophylla*	Hydrangea	
Hydrangea paniculata*	Panicled hydrangea	
Hypericum sp.	Hypericum	St John's wort
Ixodia sp.	South Australian daisy	Australian daisy
Ixodia achilleoides	Immortelle	
Juncus sp.	Rush	
Kunzea sp.	Kunzea	
Lachnostachys sp.	Lachnostachys	
Lagurus ovatus*	Lagurus	Hare's-tail grass/ bunny tails
Larix sp.	Larch cone	
Lavandula spica*	Lavender	
Lepidium rurale (also known as Lupidium)	Lepidium	
Leptospermum sp.	Silver strawberry	
Leucodendron sp.	Leucodendron	
Liatris sp.*	Liatris	Blazing star/button snakeroot
Limonium sinuatum*	Statice	
Limonium suworowii*	Russian statice	Rat's tail statice/ Pink pokers
Lonas indora	Lonas	Small-headed achillea
Lunaria annua*	Honesty	
Melaleuca sp.	Melaleuca or Brunia	
Moluccella laevis*	Bells of Ireland	Shell flower
Nelumbo lucifera	Lotus flower heads	
Nervosum verticor	Nervosum	
Nigella damascena*	Nigella	Love-in-a-mist
Nigella orientalis	Nigella orientalis	
Paeonia lactiflora*	Peony	
Papaver rhoeas*	Poppy (seed head)	
Phalaris arundinacea*	Canary grass	
Phleum sp.	Timothy grass	Rats' tails
Phlomis fruticosa*	Jerusalem sage	
Phragmites australis	Reed	
Physalis alkekengi franchetti*	Physalis	Chinese lantern
Pinus sp.	Pine cone	
Pithocarpa corymbulosa*	Miniature everlasting	
Polypogon sp.	Polypogon	Hare's-foot grass
Protea sp.	Protea	Cape honey flower
Pyrus salicifolia*	Weeping pear	
Ranunculus sp.*	Buttercup	
Rosa sp.*	Rose	
Rumex sp.*	Dock or sorrel	
Ruscus sp.	Ruscus	
Salvia farinacea*	Blue salvia	
Senecio greyi*	Senecio	
Silene pendula*	Silene	Campion
Solidago sp.*	Golden rod	
Solidaster sp.	Solidaster	
Sphagnum sp.	Sphagnum moss	
Stachys lanata*	Lamb's tongue	
Stirlingia latifolia*	Stirlingia	
Triticum sp.	Wheat	
Typha sp.	Reedmace	
Verticordia brownii	Verticordia	
Verticordia ruitens	Morrison or feather flower	
Xeranthemum sp.	Silver everlasting flower	
Zea mays	Sweet corn	Maize
Zinnia sp.*	Zinnia	

INDEX